LIFE AFTER TRAUMA

Breaking the Silence

to Inspire Resilience

My Life Rewritten | Book 1

CREATED AND COMPILED BY
DR. ANDREA PENNINGTON

MAKE YOUR MARK GLOBAL

Library of Congress Cataloging-in-Publication Data
Library of Congress Control Number: 2018913446
Life After Trauma
Publisher: Make Your Mark Global, LTD
Fernley, Nevada
Pages: 207
Paperback ISBN 978-0-9994949-3-6
Ebook ISBN 978-0-9994949-6-7
Subjects: Self-help

Summary: In Life After Trauma, Dr. Andrea Pennington presents 16 real life stories of people from various backgrounds and cultures who have found unseen forces supporting, guiding and healing them in their darkest hours. These stories cover events ranging from spontaneous experiences of divine love and recovering from childhood abuse, to personal struggles with identity and life purpose. What these stories all have in common is how they demonstrate that there are healing forces within us that trauma unlocks. There is great hope and inspiration to be found here.
Printed in the USA & UK

MAKE YOUR MARK GLOBAL PUBLISHING, LTD
USA & Monaco

For information on bulk purchase orders of this book or to book Dr. Andrea or any of the authors in this book to speak at your event or on your program, call +33 06 12 74 77 09 or send an email to Andrea@MakeYourMarkGlobal.com

LIFE AFTER TRAUMA

CONTRIBUTING AUTHORS

Stephan Conradi - Karin Eke
Stine Moe Engelsrud - Anna Frostin
Caroline Hoek - Paul Luftenegger
David E. Morris - Funmi Moser
Gila Nehemia - Gazit Chaya Nkosi
Andrea Pennington - Abbie Persall
Marike Stassar - Jill Stocker
Taz Thornton - Joyce Wazirali

DEDICATION

This book is lovingly dedicated to the beautiful souls
who have endured pain & suffering due to trauma

May this book help you remember that
you are stronger than you know

May you find peace and hope
while reclaiming your resilience

Preface

The book you hold in your hands is a collection of very generous, honest stories from courageous authors. Each of them has opened up their heart to bring you insight into what led them out of pain, confusion and breakdowns into their present lives which are full of beauty, joy and light.

Because our authors are from a variety of countries and we are publishing these stories in English you may notice that the spelling of words is sometimes in British English and sometimes in American English, depending on the author's country of origin. You'll also see that some phrases they use are unique to you, as they are not always direct translations.

In light of the fact that many of our authors are not native English speakers, our team of editors has worked hard to make each story clear and full of the impact the author intended. It is our sincere hope that we have done their compelling stories justice and that you will be moved and inspired by them.

If you'd like to hear the authors in their own voice and watch as they provide context and color to how they decided that this is the time to break their silence I invite you to visit www.MyLifeRewritten.com to watch interviews conducted by the book's publisher, Dr. Andrea Pennington.

Contents

Introduction

We all experience trauma to some degree – you could say it is a part of the human experience. But when hear the word trauma, most of us think of major events like being in combat, war, witnessing or experiencing physical or sexual abuse, or losing a loved one through illness, divorce or abandonment. We don't often think of the accumulation of little painful events as traumatic, however.

For example, psychologists agree that over time, the insults one receives from a parent, a lover or authority figure, the unreciprocated attempts to receive love or affection from a parent or loved one, the repeated failures on the playground or in the boardroom can also leave us traumatized. These are the micro-traumas that we often disregard, downplay or deny, but they hurt us and can impact our overall experience of life just as much as the 'big' traumas.

Whether the large or small traumas of life, there is no doubt that trauma can have a profound and lasting effect on our lives, our thoughts and feelings, and even our physiological response to future stress. As an integrative physician, acupuncturist and meditation teacher with a particular interest in neuroscience, I have been fascinated about the human response to trauma. I've been particularly curious to understand why some people wither away after traumatic experiences and why others bounce back even stronger.

Over the last 15 years I've seen two key distinctions about trauma that inspired me to compile the stories in *Life After Trauma* for the My Life Rewritten book series. The first distinction is that in response to traumatic experiences the brain gets re-wired in several ways, which can have a detrimental effect on our health, emotional wellbeing and how we cope with future stress. The second key distinction is that the brain doesn't get stuck that way. In fact, it is more malleable than we used to think. Our brain is like plastic and we can rewire our neuronal connections again after trauma. We can even become stronger and more able to cope with what the world throws our way.

The science of neuroplasticity has shed new light on ways to cope with everyday stress such as the microtraumas of our busy, interconnected and complicated world. And due to the moldable nature of our brains allows us to repair after illness, abuse or loss, we can rise up with more strength and vitality.

The good news is that there are plenty of tools we can call on to heal from trauma including speaking up in support groups, journaling, yoga, psychotherapy, exercise, art therapy, equine therapy, acupuncture, meditation, plant medicine journeys and so many more. The reason I compiled this collection of stories is to demonstrate that many well-known methods of recovery are useful, but there are so many other ways you can heal that you may not know about. If one type of therapy didn't work for you, there are many others available, so don't give up.

We humans are built to be resilient. The underlying message of this book is that you can have a happy life after trauma. No matter how drastic your present state of being, happiness and contentment are possible for you.

I am excited to introduce you to these extraordinary authors who will give you a chance to explore how they have recovered from life's traumas with more resilience and peace than you could imagine. The stories are poignant, honest and represent a vulnerability that is deeply moving.

Be aware that some stories may provoke strong emotional re-actions. But it's not all doom and gloom. In this book, all the authors aim to inspire you to know deeply that every cloud has its silver lining. When we come through something dark, the light at the other end is all the brighter. We can learn from our experiences, grow as people, and even develop greater resilience and compassion.

Whether you are in a dark place right now, or on the road to recovery, I wish you peace and happiness. I hope you find inspiration and strength in the real-life stories that follow.

1
Surviving Suicide

Many people find the idea of suicide utterly unthinkable. Some label those who contemplate suicide or act on their suicidal ideations as selfish. But unless you've ever felt so low, so desperate, so filled with shame or self-loathing…unless you've personally experienced the anguish of not seeing a viable future for yourself, a future worth living for, a self image worth embodying, then you couldn't understand why suicide claims so many lives each day.

As hard as it is to accept, I've now met with countless survivors of suicide who say that they found themselves so wracked with emotional pain and devoid of any hope in their future that they believed suicide was their only way out. To them, suicide was actually thought of as an extreme act of self-care, not a selfish act.

Of course people who contemplate or attempt suicide think about the people we would leave behind, none of us are blind to the idea that people left behind would suffer. But some of us have actually thought that our absence from this life may truly leave the world and our families better off.

No matter what your opinions are on whether suicide is a sin, selfish or justified, please know that the thought processes and mental state we experience when we are depressed are not always rational and certainly not holistic.

And so what happens when you consider suicide, maybe even attempt it, and you survive? Three of the stories in Part 1 will explore how after after living through failed suicide attempt the authors went from *surviving* to *thriving*.

And what about the families and friends who are left to make sense of the tragic passing of a loved one who took their own life? The story of Paul Luftenegger explores how losing his father to suicide opened up his heart to God in mystical and mysterious ways and gave him ever more reason to live with passion.

No matter the source of the dark feelings that surround suicidal thoughts, whether from years of hiding sexual or emotional abuse, witnessing trauma, or being abandoned or rejected by family, I now believe that the pain and hopelessness can be transcended. I believe that there are a variety of pathways which enable us to reunite with our divinity, which allow us to return to a state of purity and wholeness, which can deliver us from emotional turmoil and hopelessness. There are multiple ways to rebound from the lowest of lows which point to a grand purpose for our lives beyond our mind's comprehension.

I do not consider suicide to be a viable option for ending the pain and suffering of life. I believe in the infinite potential for love, redemption and expansion, all of which can move us beyond our earthly anguish into a state of self-compassion and real self-love. I hope that the each of the stories in Part 1 provide that sense of hope to you too.

We take suicide very seriously, and you should to. Some behaviors may indicate that a person is at **immediate** risk for suicide.

The following three signs should prompt you to **immediately call** the a mental health professional, the police or a suicide prevention call center.

- Talking about wanting to die or to kill oneself
- Looking for a way to kill oneself, such as searching online or obtaining a gun or deadly prescription medication
- Talking about feeling hopeless or having no reason to live

Other behaviors which may also indicate a serious risk, especially if the behavior is new, has increased, and/or seems related to a painful event, loss, or change include:

- Talking about feeling trapped or in unbearable pain
- Talking about being a burden to others
- Increasing the use of alcohol or drugs
- Acting anxious or agitated; behaving recklessly
- Sleeping too little or too much
- Withdrawing or feeling isolated
- Showing rage or talking about seeking revenge
- Displaying extreme mood swings

(USA) National Suicide Prevention Lifeline:
1-800-273-TALK (8255) This is a 24-hour toll-free phone line for people in suicidal crisis or emotional distress.

An online chat option is also available at
www.suicidepreventionlifeline.org/GetHelp/LifelineChat.aspx

International Suicide Prevention Listings

www.suicide.org/international-suicide-hotlines.html

The Darkest Night of My Soul

Paul Luftenegger

O n Sunday March 6th, 2011 my beautiful, precious 56-year-old father, *Frederick Luftenegger,* who was well-liked, respected, friendly, passionate, kind, handsome, sporty, hilarious, hard-working and incredibly giving, sadly took his own life.

The suicide of my father changed my life and my trajectory forever.

We had no idea.

We were all blindsided.

We were all shocked.

For the record, my father was a beautiful man who loved living life. He loved God and had a child's heart. He lived with values and virtues that always shined through making life for others always more beautiful and more enjoyable by sharing his beautiful soul generously with the world that surrounded him. He lived the golden rules as best he could and where he faltered he was always willing to apologize for the errors and mistakes of his ways.

He loved cooking for people and making everyone feel welcome and important.

He had this magic, miraculous quality that made everyone light up.

He loved laughing and earning a living selling fresh fruits and vegetables to people as a produce manager. I often wonder how many people my father fed and nourished with good healthy food throughout his lifetime.

He was known for always finding the freshest most beautiful cornucopia of food the earth produced for those he loved most. I remember often seeing his face light up with customers that he cared for who loved sharing time with him.

I remember countless times where he would bring bags of the most in-season produce home sharing it with such passion with everyone around. Life with my dad by your side was exciting and inspired!

Sadly my father hung himself with a rope tied around his neck just a little more than 1 month before his 57th birthday. In my family suicide repeated itself. My father's father had also taken his own life by suicide when my dad was only 9 years old. My grandfather jumped from a huge railway trestle leaving his wife and 3 children behind – my dad was one of those children – the oldest boy.

My dad's last footprint in life would literally be the last step that killed him. The fact that he knew he would die that night is such a haunting space for me because his *goodbye* and his *goodnight wishes* were given to me with a knowingness of his coming death – he knowing it was coming – and me knowing nothing about it. This is the part of suicide that torments those left behind, the helplessness and hopelessness when someone you love with all your heart and soul chooses to die. Losing the will and the desire to live is a brutal truth of mental health issues. I have sadly seen this truth too many times to count.

I remember so clearly that last night of my father's life – he had washed all of his clothes. He made us a simple dinner to share time together and right before heading to bed he took a shower and with his pink, clean skin, he came to me to say goodnight. I remember so clearly how he took an extra pause to look at me with an inward reflection, smiling at me with his kind soft gaze illuminating from his soul. He told me that he loved me, and smiled with a warmth of what I now know was his way of saying goodbye.

I also remember him in the laundry room earlier that night, seeing him floss his teeth with such determination. I remember him coming into the T.V. room telling me that he had to get up early to do "paperwork" and that he would try to be as quiet as possible to make sure he didn't wake my mom or me in the wee hours of the morning. He had become so thoughtful in the last years of his life; another quality I treasure deeply.

From what we could tell the rope was fixed to a cold steel beam in the garage of my parents home where I grew up and became me.

My father died surrounded by his two favourite things – his boat and his motorcycles. I will never forget what it looks like or feels like to see and experience finding the man who gave me the gift and miracle of my own life – murdered by his own two hands, abandoning and jumping ship on the life we shared together. It was a great life and sadly the truth is – he didn't want to be in it any longer. The hardest part of suicide is the feeling of being abandoned.

What I know now is that famous question *"how many times do you have to die before you truly live"* is so profound, so important, and so vital to understand. I promised myself the day my father died that I would live my love to life and not let his life be in vain.

I will always remember what it feels like to hear my mother's primal scream – I have never heard this type of scream from anyone – and I hope to never hear anything resembling its frequency again.

I will always remember what it feels like to call 911 on the telephone. I remember trying to avoid looking out the windows to see what the emergency crews were doing – Police, Fire, Ambulance, Coroner, Forensic Unit – all the emergency vehicles red and white lights flashing and reflecting on the fresh white snow. All the men and women surrounding us with support – all the Angels there to help us in our time of need. The chaos. The confusion. The sadness. The shock.

It is a morning that is carved and etched in my memory like a Michelangelo sculpture in Rome with such specific fine details; the anatomy of suicide.

The line that divides the *"knowing"* and the *"not knowing"* he was dead – is such a distinctive precise space – a space I will always understand which delineated the old me from the new me.

The Not Knowing

I remember the miraculous soft beautiful snow that night; it stuck to everything in its path and it sparkled with blinding diamond lights that morning on March 6th.

I remember the thick, heavenly, mystical alchemy of the angelic balm of pure divine holy love in the air – the beauty of the calm before the horrendousness of the suicide storm.

I remember the magical feeling of being home with both my mom and my dad together for the last time on that early Sunday morning, thinking that my father was sleeping in and resting – enjoying the wonder of a cozy winter's Sunday morning at home with family and time off to enjoy life together.

I remember falling head over heels in love with Adele's new release "Someone Like You" that week – listening to it over and over again with goosebumps, falling in love with Adele more each time. I had actually played it for the first time to my mother that morning and she loved it so much that she asked me to play it a 2ⁿᵈ time while both sipped a morning cup of coffee together. I remember feeling how precious and sacred it was to share music that I loved with my mom. It was something we always did when we found a song we loved.

True Healing Takes Listening to God from Within

The morning my father died I collapsed in my grief – I began imploding into myself just like a skyscraper being demolished with dynamite in an organized planned demolition. I remember thinking, "God can this be real?"

I have never been so afraid of anything in my whole life. My heart broke into billions and billions of fragmented pieces – shards of what once was – I had so much pain welling up that I could barely breathe or talk.

I remember starting to hyperventilate, not wanting the police officer questioning me to notice my physical distress. I remember thinking I was going to die and lose consciousness with my heart and soul's pain being far too great for my body to physically handle. I remember so clearly whispering to God from within,

> "God, I need your help right now, I am not big enough to do this anymore, I am so scared, I am so afraid, I am hurting too much, please, please, please help me – help me... I am not ok right now…I need you God… please help me!"

What happened next is what changed my life forever! God came to me and told me with my inner voice that I was going to be OK and that there would be blessings that would come from this horrendous tragedy. God said so specifically,

"I am with you Paul. You are not alone. You have never been alone. I have always been with you and I would never leave or abandon you, my precious child. I am here for you and I will help you each step of the way. Come be with me and I will help you."

A holy feeling washed over my whole body and although I was still in pain I was in awe of knowing I was not alone and that God was with me to help me through.

The feeling of knowing this is what makes me cry – you see, my life changed on a dime from that prayer to God. I knew the feeling of God's divine, holy love and sacred heart being inside of my own heart. It is God's love that has healed me, and the fact I was not alone is what makes my heart well with gratitude. My pain lessened enough that I could breathe again.

God has been with me each day since March 6th – refreshing and refuelling my whole sovereign being in knowing that I am ok and that all is well and that all shall always be well with God, from the inside out.

What is so miraculous all these 7 years, 7 months, and 8 days later is that I started to follow God's plan for me from the inside out – healing the past and listening to my inner technology and guidance. The inner voice of my being came online with God's divine, holy love and sacred plan. Each day I left space for God through meditation and prayer to be inside of myself and to see what was surfacing and coming into focus. I was told by God many times in my healing practice that I will never have peace in my life until I find and make peace from within myself.

What is so interesting is that in 2011 Oprah Winfrey ended her daytime talk show and the same year she started her new network called "OWN." I remember God guiding me to pay attention to the shows on the OWN network.

I watched a show that changed my life forever, *"Master-Class"*. God guided me to watch an episode featuring Dr. Maya Angelou sharing her life story. Maya was once a mute because she thought that by speaking up her words had killed a man who raped her when she was a young child. For 6 years Maya didn't speak. Maya taught me that words have power and one must choose their words wisely as one day words will be able to be measured for how much power each word holds.

These two beautiful Angels, Maya and Oprah, were sent to my door by God to watch and learn from. They were sent to help me heal; an answer to my prayers.

What I understand now is that the most important decision any of us can make is to follow Einstein's advice: to choose whether we live in a hostile or a loving Universe. I have always known that I live in a loving Universe with God's infinite, pure holy love. I know that if one chooses anything but a loving universe then that very thing surrounds them. I feel completely wrapped in the loving vibrations and frequencies of God and each day I honour this by living a mantra that God showed me – to literally be *"Love Expanding Love"* – in full manifestation. To ultimately be the love I wish to experience in the world by co+creating this love and frequency with others.

Soon after I was visited by God again at the piano and was told that I would write music to help the world forever. I remember at the time being upset with God for making this statement to me; I told God that God had the wrong person and would have to find someone else.

I remember God just smiling at me, saying nothing with a totally peaceful presence of grace.

What is so funny, looking back at all of this now, 6 conscious albums later, is that music and God helped me to heal my whole heart, soul, and spirit. And no matter what I did to deny this truth I couldn't refuse this fact if I tried.

What I know for sure is that God has a plan for each and every one of us and it involves us surrendering with full commitment. God is always there for us in Omnipresent love and the inner technology is where each of us will find God's divine love waiting patiently for our highest self to beam to life.

Our sacred heart in harmony with God's sacred heart is what sets our soul free to shine with divine love. Letting go of all limiting beliefs is, in fact, the way home.

God is patiently waiting for us to fill our entire being with this infinite, holy, sacred vibrational beauty. The frequencies of heaven are pure love and our only job is to fill our whole being with this divine love each day through our spiritual practice.

I like to see the sacred heart inside myself as a holy chalice. I know that bringing God's pure holy divine love and light; the nectar of heaven, through our crown, down to our third eye, down through our throat, and then down into our sacred heart chalice is what allows the Aura of God to fill our entire Lightbody. Filling our holy chalice (our heart) and letting this heavenly nectar overflow into our life is in fact how we truly heal and how become the light of God manifest in physical form.

What we must all come to terms with is the eternal soul and its original pure sacred light of holy love. It is the heart and soul that powers the body, much like a car. Without the car having a heart or soul there is no driver to drive the vehicle.

This is how I see things and understand what happened to me; I finally understood that I am my eternal, sacred, divine, loving holy soul driving my body consciously.

What is amazing all these years later is that my music has taken me to the United Nations Headquarters in New York City

3 times as an invited guest. I have sung my conscious songs for the UN International Day of Yoga, The UN International Day of Women, and The UN International Day of Peace.

My music has been used to honour the life of the amazing late great Louise Hay for her last birthday in front of 2000 people in San Diego ,California.

My music has been contracted by *"So You Think You Can Dance"* and taken me on missions to help people in need receive free hearing aids with the *Starkey Hearing Foundation.*

I have worked with many New York Times best selling authors and been invited to travel to far away places like India, Spain, England, the USA and more to sing my conscious songs to help hearts and souls.

My conscious music is used in classrooms all over the world and in clinics by therapists to help bring attention to the importance of self-love and self-worth.

My music has been used by countless suicide awareness campaigns and I have been interviewed on several public broadcasting stations to share the holy spirit of togetherness, inspiring global love and kindness from within.

These blessings have taught me that our beliefs, thoughts and frequencies create the life we live. I know with absolute certainty that the energy you put out comes back to you and what you seek you definitely find – because what you seek is always seeking you. I also know for sure that the whispers of God are found on the inside of you and it is through prayer and meditation that God is able to help each of us develop the intimate sacred relationship with our source.

If you truly want the heaven of your life on earth you must surrender to God because no one is big enough to do this alone. No one. Not you. Not me. No one.

What is the most fascinating thing I have learned since my father died is that if you want more love, more happiness, or more joy in your life you must take full responsibility for the energy you create and put out in every single moment. If you want to have love in your life you must love more. If you want more joy in your life you must create more joyful moments. If you want more happiness in your life you must create and co+create with other happy people!

I personally feel that cynicism, negativity, and the inability to forgive others are the most self-harming choices we can make. I also know that we are just like a microphone and what we amplify becomes manifest. Amplify bad and bad will surround you. Amplify good and good will surround you.

I also know without any doubt that self worth and self love are the only way to truly thrive in this new world. I also know that God loves you so very much and because you are here you matter!

To end, I recently heard Whoopi Goldberg share a statement with a good friend, Dr. Sister Jenna, that I love to ponder,

"When we live the golden rules to life isn't it then that we're in heaven?"

About the Author

Paul Luftenegger is an International Multi Award Winning Singer, Songwriter, and Composer. Paul writes conscious music to inspire and promote global love and kindness from within. Paul's focus is nurturing self worth within the listener. He has performed for the United Nations 3 times and his music has been used to honour icons like Louise Hay.

Paul serves the "Starkey Hearing Foundation" helping to give free hearing aids to those in need around the world. His song Diamond Light won the 'Honourable Mention Award' from the USA International Songwriting Competition in 2013 and the album of the same name, the Top 10 Award by the London Free Press. Paul's music is used in classrooms worldwide to help children understand the importance of self-love and self kindness. Paul tours with his music and provides healing workshops around the globe – singing, speaking, and teaching.

Paul Luftenegger's Albums:

1. Beautiful World / Blessings From Above
2. Worthy
3. Diamond Light
4. Love Expanding Love
5. The Miracle of You
6. Faith

www.beekindness.com
Email: info@paulluftenegger.com
Facebook.com/luftenegger
Twitter.com/luftenegger
Instagram.com/paulandcori

In This Body

Gazit Chaya Nkosi

"My body is but wax and wick for flame. When the candle burns out, the Light shines elsewhere."
~ Egyptian Book of the Dead

We have been given and taken on many physical bodies, 'I'dentities and labels. In this body, I've been given many, some of which are: suicide survivor, disabled, cisgender, female, brilliant, brain-injured, divorced, daughter, lesbian, poor, educated, survivor, wife, Jew, bipolar, mom, sensitive, white, radical, borderline, activist, pervert, privileged, sister, Christ-like, mentally ill, relative of alcoholics, addicts, and abusers, and most often just 'too much.'

None of these are relevant to the divinity which I seek to cultivate in my daily life and, for that reason, I am often drawn by a longing to be out of this body and revel in the Light shining elsewhere. However, there were times when I felt forced to be only the body, and it is for that self and time that I write.

Decades were oppressed by blame, shame, comparison and victim thinking. The initial attempts to leave this hell were a frantic grasping. I performed simple actions I had been told would lead me into "a life worth living." I turned on the faucet to allow cold water to trigger a reflex to calm my fight or flight response. I breathed shakily in for 4, held for 7 and out for 8. I listened warily to 5 minute guided meditations. I begrudgingly wrote a gratitude list. And with these banal actions, done in skepticism and desperation, I emerged slowly but surely into the light of Life once more.

But first came the darkness.

"Had I not fallen, I would not have arisen.
Had I not been subject to darkness,
I could not have seen the Light."
~ Midrash

At 22 years of age, I felt proud of my first solo apartment. I carefully cleaned and organized the space, envisioning it through my mother's eyes. With each corner swept, no dirty remnants in the sink or laundry bin, with the picture frames aligned just so, I relaxed into the comfort of knowing they would not have to clean. I chose new, modest pajamas, those who carried me out would feel no discomfort or shame in seeing my sleeping state. I unplugged the phone, laid carefully into the smoothly straightened sheets, and slowly swallowed the multi-colored pills. The larger white ones were chalky and bitter. The small, pink ones were mildly sweet, dissolving slightly on my warm tongue. The peace and assurance of giving salvation to my loved ones through this sacrifice embraced me like the lightest duvet of comfort, enveloping me in pure bliss. The room faded and I sighed wholly into the infinite, dissolved of it all, held sweetly by the joy of giving this final gift.

The clattering of medical equipment, the glare of fluorescent lights and the charcoal, gritty between my teeth, suctioned me violently back out.

"I need floss!" I screeched in disoriented panic.

My teeth stretched painfully and my lips cracked as the black grit was forced into my mouth. My friend pulled a long, glistening, brown hair from her head and I sighed with relief as it slipped between my aching teeth.

And then it struck me, slamming shut like shackles around my wrists. I recoiled in disgust and shame fell over me in the heaviness of sackcloth and ashes. Once again, I was alive.

"My direction has shifted. From being ignant and gifted, suicidal and explicit. To being humbly committed, and preferably submissive to the source of all existence. I value my life more than ever."
~ Georgia Anne Muldrow

Life. She has relentlessly pursued me, crept behind me as I tried to walk away aloof and indifferent. My shoulders tense, my heart still, I brace myself and she pounces. My heart screeches as I feel her claws slice through my skin, again and again we repeat our dance.

At first it was awkward, sometimes flattering. She kept asserting and pushing up against me. I tried to be subtle, politely decline. She found me everywhere, and the pursuit intensified.

"I don't even know you," I told her. "Please stop," I asked. "Get thee behind me," I pronounced and still she found me. Again and again.

And then one day, I submitted. Spiraling down and down as this pursuer stalked me into insanity, there was no way to outthink or outsmart this force. Finally and finally I gave in to be washed away and through, a high pitch ringing in the empty room, the black encircled and closed in and around me. Silence, silence, nothing. How familiar this is, how endless this cycle.

The red hum pulls me out of the darkness. The rough, grey rock that was, has finally broken. It has opened into two pieces and within it is a geode, the room sparkles with fractals of rainbow light.

"It is finished."
~ Jesus of Nazareth

I tried to put the geode back together. To pretend she was never here. But once it opened, it would never close. She was there constantly. In the beginning it was uncomfortable, back against the wall, I half-smiled. She offered me luxury and opulence, I yearned for lack. She caressed me deeply, I pulled away, craving the sting of a slap. She bowed before me and claimed my divinity, I recoiled from this most of all.

Beside me she walks. But it is different now, the intensity is gone. She no longer stalks, pushes, torments. One day, I lifted a corner of the sackcloth and peeked. Was it she who had transformed or I? With deep, luminous, never ending, crystalline blackness she glows, a sphere of glistening onyx, endlessly rotating, reflecting back on endless repeat her message, "choose life, choose life, choose life."

"You do not have to be good. You do not have to walk on your knees for a hundred miles through the desert, repenting. You only have to let the soft animal of your body love what it loves..."
~ Mary Oliver

Raised in the church, idolizing martyrs and saints, my surest desire was to be good. The stories spiraled my hopes upward into the promise of heaven and the assurance of salvation from hell. I knew the rules and for years they were easy to follow. At 12, I fell flat with the realization that great spirituality most often arose out of the deepest wells of suffering and yet I could find none.

I had money, beauty, intelligence and spiritual integrity and understanding beyond the sages I had read and yet I yearned for something deeper still.

I committed myself through prayer and petition to the one desire, "Lord make me uncomfortable, that I may see Your face."

How quickly He answered. And the answer matched the request in perfect and harmonious vibration.

She was leaning down and slowing sliding her shorts up her smoothly shaven legs. Her delicate fingers, with the smudge of grey pencil lead on her pinky, deftly buttoned her shorts beneath her creamy navel. My eyes followed up to the silken floral that cradled her blossoming breasts.

I walked slowly from the locker room, each step heavy with knowledge and purpose, to return to my classes. I was gay. This was God's answer. He had awakened me to the thorn in my side, my spiritual cross to bear and I accepted it with gratitude. By the time I reached the classroom door, I was confidently robed in my battle gear with my enemy clearly defined. My chest swollen with the pride of purpose, I entered confidently into the fight.

"You are a whispering diamond, turning in the sun, articulating the one thing the sky wants to say, in a million different ways."
~ Curtis Tyrone Jones

I kneeled at her side, as she shook and writhed, clammy and pale at the confession. We had returned to school, all thoroughly shaken by the events of 9/11, each searching for answers to our deepest questions. When we had met a few weeks ago she had been strong, arrogant even in her tale of her lesbian love, unapologetic as she described her ravishing girlfriend. But now those same strong shoulders sank as she described her commitment to leave this life behind. My skin began to crawl as I heard her. I was witnessing myself in her and as she spoke I felt her take the whip of self-hatred and self-abandonment and pull it slowly across both our backs.

In the communal sadness left by the tragedy, she had followed some friends to a revival. The crusaders used the collective fear to capture her soul. They promised her hope and life and salvation and love. In return, she owed them her body, her desire, her sexuality. She gave herself to Jesus, she told me. He would save her from the unnatural perversions of herself and lead her into resurrection.

Until then, I had carried the assurance of the perversion of my homosexuality as a badge of honor. I was proud of my martyrdom, and self-righteous in the greatness of my task. But that day, in her agony, I saw my reflection and a whisper of light slipped through. I was shocked by the realization of what I had done. I reached in desperation to remove the cross from her shoulders, I screamed with the Messiah in despair, "My God, My God, why have you forsaken her?"

"I have asked heaven and earth to witness today, I have set before you, a choice you must make. Life or death, blessings or curses, the choice is up to you. And so I ask you know, what will you do? Choose life, that you might

live, you and your people, choose life, that you might live, close to God, choose life that you might live, you and your people, choose life, that you might live with God."
~ Deuteronomy 30:19

And in that moment the geode was exposed. Did I choose Life, did she choose me, was it consensual? In many iterations, it seemed she yanked me out of the drowning waters against my will. Sometimes I fought, sometimes I gave in. At times, I felt guilty, why was I chosen while others slipped down in the cold waters of death.

In the end, I gave into her, and no longer ask her to convince me. She has offered, I have received. I can no longer question my worth or the decision, I have been chosen and have accepted. She threw me up against the wall, and at long last I let her consume me again and again until I sink with satisfied exhaustion into the strength of her arms.

At last we have committed to one another, entangled in the ecstasy of all that is. She wakes me up with soft, ripe, kisses of morning light. Her eyes twinkle at me in the shimmering wooshing of fluttering leaves. My body throbs, pulses and exhales as her passion washes over me in the laughter of children, the fierce courage of mothers, and the surprising tenderness of a man sharing honestly. When I question if she is still there and if she *truly* wants *me*, her soft hand reassures me in the screech of a blue jay, the soaring silhouette of a hawk, or the voice of my daughter calling my name.

"They may
defeat you,

burn you,

insult you,

injure you,

and abandon you,

but they

will not

shall not

and cannot

destroy you,

for you,

like Rome,

were built on ashes,

and you,

like a phoenix,

know how to resurrect."

~ Nikita Gill

And now, dear soul, I offer you to follow me with gentle, hesitant tiptoes into the light of Life as she holds out her hand to us both. We were brought into the darkness so that we might recognize Her. But precious one, we were never meant to stay in the darkness for long. I hold out my hand and offer to walk beside you on your way. Life, my lover, she is a gentle teacher, but her harsh hand only turns to caresses when you surrender your warm body into her embrace. One millisecond at a time, through tiny physical actions, may you come to experience this unconditional joy and light which is never-ceasing and all around us.

You are not alone, we can expose and embrace the divinity of Life and let go of the lies of fear, guilt and shame together. And so, it is.

About the Author

Gazit Chaya Nkosi is taking steps out of her old paradigm and into something new. Part of this journey is the offering of The Luria Center, a place for individuals who desire to move out of desperation and into a life of fulfillment and unconditional joy. The Luria uses a peer-coaching model and offers specific skills and strategies to manage painful emotions, decrease conflict in relationships, develop mindfulness, and "live a life worth living" based on values rather than outcomes. The model is centered on the teachings of Dialectical Behavioral Therapy, mindfulness, and functional psychology, along with ancient, sacred texts and spiritual practices.

You are welcome to visit The Luria and explore if our community is right for you: www.theluria.mn.co

Gazit Chaya lives in Amherst, MA with her ethereal child and their beloved cat, guardian and guide, Sandy.

Join her at: www.gazitchayankosi.com.

Me + Him + Her

David E. Morris

Feeling

The "black hole" has returned.

The unmistakable numbness where I can smell the fear and confusion and I can feel it slowly creeping inside me. I can taste the sickness and I can almost touch its layers. And yet, I feel nothing.

The quicksand sinking feeling of struggle has returned. I'm drowning in the darkness. My mind is struggling for control. He is here.

No matter how hard I have tried to fight it. No matter how much I have tried to heal from within. No matter where I tried to hide. He has found me once again. He has come to reclaim my soul and drive me down the dark path of destruction, to finish my existence where he failed so many years before.

I thought I had learned my life's lesson, back in 2010, when I tried to take my own life and ended up in a psychiatric hospital tied to a bed. Scared, angry, and hooked up to breathing machine, I was in a drug induced parallel world for about six days in a psychiatric hospital. It was the aftermath of my first suicide attempt and it was a place I promised myself I would never go back.

Apparently, I forget rather easily. Because quickly I returned "to life" under the illusion that I would be fine.

I listened to all the therapists, I went to my scheduled appointments and I told them my truth about the suicide attempt. But today I wonder, if maybe, just maybe I told them what they wanted to hear so that I could be left alone in my guilt and embarrassment.

I told everyone, including my family, that I was going to be OK, that the first time was just a fluke, a stupid mistake, nothing but a horrible lapse in judgment. I promised myself, my therapists, my friends, my family, and later on I even promised her, it would never ever happen again.

I chose to believe, that I was now much stronger inside and would always ask for help if I ever felt that worthless again. If I ever felt I was succumbing to my demons.

I swore that if I ever lost my will to live, I would find my way towards help, and reach out in any way I could. But here I am once again... Here I am.

Taking Action

I felt the raw desperation intensify... and that's when he whispered in my ear;

"See, I told you you are a horrible person and father."

"You, don't deserve love."

"You...DON'T deserve to exist!"

"Go ahead loser, finish what you couldn't the first time. I will help you this time, you fucking coward!"

My head was spinning, I felt like I couldn't breathe as the world around me started to crumble once again.

As the clock read 14:30, I calmly walked into my office and reached into the office gift cabinet. I pulled out a bottle of whiskey, put it in my backpack, then slowly walked out the front door without saying a word to anyone. I had absolutely no idea where I was going or what I was doing, so I just kept walking. Thinking about the people I loved and how I had let them down over and over.

My close encounter with suicide years before had really helped put my life in perspective and I had tried to respect myself and my boundaries. But, once he grabbed ahold of my thoughts, everything else seemed to become irrelevant.

I walked through traffic without looking for speeding cars. I walked through a beautiful park without looking at a single beautiful flower or hearing any birds singing. I can't remember looking at one single face walking through the park that day. I was looking *through* people not at them, almost as if I was in a zombie trance. I was on a mission.

He was luring me towards my demise.

I could smell the salt air getting closer as I stumbled slowly, yet calmly past the park. Although I was unsure where I was headed, the scent of the salty breeze drove me toward it.

"There," he said to me, "just keep going towards the water."

The smell of the ocean comforted me. It spoke to me of my many years at sea with the U.S. Navy. Yes, it made sense to me. He was right. He was always right. I had to return to the sea.

As the docks opened wide in front of me, I tasted the salt and heard the seagulls. The large shipping canal made the water a dark, deep hue of blue in front of me. I passed by two fishermen who were minding their own business, not paying me any attention. I could feel the wind against my face. It felt wonderful against my skin, I felt at home, I felt safe. I was ready.

My spot on the pier was very secluded. Far away from the fishermen, and far away from anyone else's view. Nobody would find me or disturb me. So I sat down on the pier and opened my bottle of whiskey. The first sip was exhilarating. He must be pleased to feel the alcohol from within.

Drink after drink I sat there, swig after swig I spoke to myself as I contemplated what my next pain-numbing move would be. As I looked down into the water, I could see my blurry reflection through the small waves of the canal, when suddenly his voice seemed to enter my thoughts.

"Take all 100 Valium pills out of the box in your backpack and wash them down with all the sweet whiskey you can and when you feel the rush of calmness inside you, just slowly and quietly slip into the water and never feel the pain again my friend."

This was how I could finally and gently make all the hurt stop manifesting from within. I could silence him once and for all!

Dying

I woke up that morning feeling both loved, sad, and terrified inside. I didn't quite know what to do with myself and what to make of my anxious thoughts.

It's almost as if I felt guilty inside for feeling love again and starting a new life with my true soulmate and best friend, with whom I had now lived for about 3 months. She was someone who I felt connected to since the first day we met. She was someone I felt I had known my whole life and maybe even in a past life.

She was someone so special that she lit up a room with just her presence, and when she spoke, all ears listened to what she said. She never judged me for any of my horrible and embarrassing life decisions, she always believed in me and loved me for just being me!

Although I had escaped from my torturous past and a marriage filled with lies, deceit, manipulation, and my wife's opioid addiction, I still felt very unbalanced in my new life. My work life suffered horribly. You wouldn't have known it, but my confidence level and self-esteem were lower than ever.

The guilt of moving my young son away and leaving my older daughter to fend for herself with an incapable mother was a lot for my soul to bear. Growing up as a codependent child myself, I understood why my daughter 'couldn't' leave her mother, no matter how bad everyday life had gotten. I too had lived that childhood.

So, while I was happy to be out of my old life, living in a new city, and very much in love with my soulmate, I was still suffering inside by not being honest with myself about just how low and lost I was truly feeling inside. I never should have ignored the pain and kept pushing through like nothing was wrong. I did have a choice to ask for help, admitting that I felt overwhelmed and tired inside. But I didn't do it.

Going through divorce was extremely hard. The disappointment, the failure, guilt, and emotional roller coaster seemed never ending. But going through a one-sided divorce as I did, where communication was translated into threats, shaming and more threats, was extremely damaging for me and my mental health. My daughter felt like she had to choose sides and kept communication with me to a minimum to avoid conflict and drama with her mother. She showed loyalty to the parent she was living with at the time.

I tried so hard to keep my daughter safe from the wrath of my divorce. My guilt in not being able to regularly talk to my oldest child was heartbreaking. I was now living an hour away from her and had no daily influence. So my ex-wife was free to paint whatever picture she wanted and simultaneously aimed the threats and guilt trips directly at, and into, my very vulnerable soul.

I was texting my daughter regularly. Sending her messages asking if we could talk in person, so we could re-establish our relationship. I hoped that we could soon visit each other and talk face to face. We were facing difficult challenges by living in separate locations. I just wanted my daughter to be happy and for her to know that I truly missed and loved her, I desperately wanted contact with my little girl.

I had no desire to work that day. I never should have gone. I was tired inside my head, I felt weak, and I had no business going in.

I had a supervisor that constantly reminded me of my ex-wife because she possessed the same manipulative and narcissistic behaviors and communication that tore my marriage apart. So I felt triggered. Triggered and vulnerable, even at work.

I hadn't received any messages all morning from my daughter and was starting to feel very empty inside.

Where is she? I wondered. What is she doing? Is she mad at me for leaving? When will I be able to see her again?

As my lunch hour arrived I didn't feel much like eating, food seemed irrelevant to me, I just wanted to smoke a Marlboro and sit outside on a bench with my thoughts away from my desk, away from everyone.

As I was sitting on the bench barely half way through my cigarette, I received a phone call. The caller I.D. showed the call was from my ex-wife. Agghhh!!! What did she want now? I was already having a shit day and now was getting calls at work from my embittered ex! How could this day get any worse? What the hell was happening?

The phone call with my ex was excruciating. The call ended with my ex telling me that my daughter didn't want me to contact her anymore. She didn't want to see me again and our father-daughter relationship would never be the same. She added, that they were moving to the other side of the country approximately 4 hours away.

I was in total shock.

I couldn't believe those words were actually coming from my little girl and somewhere in my soul I knew, that what I was being told was more lies and manipulations. I should have never believed, but I had become accustomed to the emotional abuse.

I was very vulnerable. I was weak and tired of constantly being on guard.

Living

As I sat on the dock I continued to take sips from my whiskey bottle. As I unwrapped each individual Valium pill, slowly and methodically, I would take one out and then take a drink of my new favorite beverage.

Over and over I continued this new ritual while creating a large circle with my bottle of 100 pills I had just refilled a day before. When the circle of Valium pills was finally completed and with more than half my bottle of whiskey now depleted, I was now ready to finally put all this pain to rest, to feel the real peace I had been looking for but failed to find the last time he really spoke to me.

As I slowly swallowed my last drink from my bottle and gathered my handful of pills, everything around me seemed to be moving in slow motion. The waves below me moved silently and the seagull's howls sounded muffled, I reminded myself how much I loved the ocean as a sailor and now I could rest there forever.

Before I raised my handful of pills towards my mouth, I looked at the water one last time and prayed to my God, "Thank you for helping me find love, thank you for my children, please take care of them for me and let them know how much I love them, please let her know she is loved. But I know that don't deserve them..."

As I finished my prayer, the calling grew louder and I felt it through my very bones. Death was calling me, he was calling me home.

Suddenly. Tires screeching. The sounds of a car engine. Somewhere right behind me.

I could smell the asphalt and tire rubber burning in the air. A car door was thrust opened behind me and I could hear and feel feet running towards me. I wasn't quite sure what was happening. Someone was gasping for air in a panic and moving quickly towards me. Had the fishermen seen what I was doing?

Had my God decided to intervene and spare my life once again?

Then I heard her scream, "Dave!"

As I felt the warmth of arms wrapping themselves around me from behind, I dropped my handful of pills into the water and watched them slowly sink to the bottom.

I could feel her. I could smell her. I felt safe with her.

And as I sat in utter shock, tears rolled down my eyes. We held each other and cried together. I felt her love again, and I felt whole. I felt worthy.

Suddenly, he was gone.

It was her.
The one that took all the pain I had away.

It was her.
The one with special powers to heal and nurture.

It was her.
The one that my soul met so many centuries ago.
The one that gave me the strength within to keep on living.
The one that froze time and allowed me into her soul.

IT WAS HER

About the Author

David E. Morris is a 22 Year Military Veteran and advocate for suicide prevention and depression awareness for both military and civilians alike.

David is from the Detroit metro area and currently resides in Denmark with his wife and 3 children.

Dave is currently working on his first solo book entitled *"The Birch Tree"* about his traumatizing childhood and first suicide attempt and survival.

Contact David by email at districtd@icloud.com
Instagram.com/district_d
Facebook.com/districtd11

I Am Woman

Caroline Hoek

The doorbell rang.

"Go away," I shouted. "Go away!" I sat in silence on the floor, back against the wall. With the oven door open, the geyser flame off, gas filled the kitchen. I could smell it. I had carefully blocked the kitchen door and ventilation system so no oxygen would flow in to slow down the process. All I had to do was wait.

Devoured by guilt and shame. Not worthy of love. I longed for death. I longed for the moment that all would stop.

How it All began

I have never been really carefree. I thought I could be, if maybe I had money. Money would buy me freedom, I thought. Struggling, feeling insecure, insufficient, I quit school. No matter how I tried to relax, fear was with me constantly. Exams made me sick to the stomach. I felt I was being weighed, measured and found wanting.

"You are not using your gifts, Caroline."
"You could have done better, Caroline."
"If only you had put in more effort…"
Words used by parents and teachers alike.
I dropped out.

I discovered men liked my body at the age of 10, when the abuse started. Even my teacher liked my tiny breasts, barely able to fit a training bra. The way he looked at me gave me the shivers.

But at the age of 23, I decided it was my turn: "You men who think you can dominate. Now I'm calling the shots."

I became a whore.

The brothel was on the other side of town. Not knowing what I should wear, I put some clothes and underwear in a bag. I decided to go by bike, needing some time to relax, I was more nervous than expected.

It was late summer. The water in the canal appeared almost golden from the sun's reflection. Parents and small children fed the ducks. They seemed happy, but looks can be deceiving.

"Who would guess I am on my way to a whorehouse?" I wondered, when the interview came back to mind. I enjoyed our conversation on the phone. It was effortless and yet no-nonsense. The woman on the other end didn't ask about frivolous things as the others had, such as the colour of my hair.

"Come just the way you are," she had said. "You will be working with only 3 other women. We like to keep it simple".

There was no bar in which I had to seduce men into drinking champagne, before enticing them in going to a room. All customers just came in and would take their pick. I tried to picture it but since this was all new, I had no idea what to expect. Taking the back entrance as instructed, I saw a casually dressed woman making tea. The man sitting at the kitchen table stood up and approached me with an outstretched hand.

"You must be Caroline." He said with a firm handshake. "Nice to meet you. Wowzers, you are looking good!"

'So far so good', I thought as I shyly thanked him for the compliment. His name was Paul. The woman was introduced as Annie, the Madam.

I followed her to the living room where the other women were. The room had two leather couches and a few chairs covered with flowery drapes; they would have suited my grandmother's house. The gold and greenish wallpaper matched the golden lamps adorned with teardrop shaped glass pendants. The wooden floor was covered with red carpet.

At the table sat two scantily dressed women who looked up as we entered. The woman named Rita said she would show me the ropes.

There were three regular bedrooms, 2 with a bath. "If you can get them to take this room they pay more money," she explained. The room with the locked door was for the mistress, who only worked during the evenings. I was supposed to work during the day but was intrigued by what might go on behind that door.

"So," Rita said, "the one thing you should bear in mind is that before taking the Johns to bed you have to wash them. Here are the towels, see? Those you keep at the sink."

She pointed at the little black ones.

"And those you take with you in the bed to prevent staining."

Just a few more things I needed to know then I could change into the blue body stocking I brought. Before I finished drinking my tea, a man in his fifties walked in. Rita and Mary assumed sexy poses as if on cue, pushing their tits slightly forward and curving their backs. This game was new to me. But as I was new, the man's gaze turned to me.

"I don't know you, young lady, what is your name?"

Not really paying attention to my answer, he announced he wanted me.

"For how long?", the Madam wanted to know. My first half hour was booked.

After closing the door, I asked him to take off his clothes. Taking the small towel, I was ready to do as Rita had instructed. I wasn't very skilled in putting on a condom, but when it was in place, all I had to do was spread my legs.

My mind wandered off while he was on top of me, breathing heavily. I was surprised with how easy the deed was done. He wanted to chat a little. Told me about his pigeons and left.

It turned out to be the routine throughout that first day. Being the 'new face' most men chose me.

After I earned my first check I invited my boyfriend out to dinner. Although he was pleased to see me, he did not welcome me with the kiss I longed for.

"Sorry, Caroline. Of course, I respect your choice, but I have to find my way in this too." Not showing my disappointment, I replied with a short 'Sure'. I stayed the night, but even there the sweetness was absent.

Soon the excitement was gone. I was bored with the men who so easily were fooled with my, "Oh, you are great. Yes, go on, I am coming. You are the best." My contempt was never seen. But a few of them I actually liked. Some so good looking, young and kind I truly questioned why they came to me.

I hated the ones who would call their wives, saying the meeting lasted longer than expected, whilst undressing me with a horny look. But I would play the game of the longing mistress, only to manipulate him into leaving a big tip.

My days had become predictable. Tall, short, fat, skinny, from senior citizens to university professors. Cocks with different skin, size and shapes, I had seen them all. Slowly it started to dawn on me that after spending time here they all went back to work, wives, and friends. Probably not giving me a second thought.

No longer the 'new face', over time I had to compete with the others. Again, I felt insecure and insufficient. Again, I was being weighed and measured.

Who am I kidding, thinking I am calling the shots?

The Tide Turns

Summer soon turned to autumn. The leaves fell from the trees as a soft evening breeze gently brushed my cheeks.

I have been working late and longed for my bed. My footsteps echo in the narrow streets. With a full moon guiding my way, the stillness of it all makes it almost magical.

As I approach the park I hesitate for a moment. Should I go in? Not wanting to make a detour I decide to walk on. As I speed up my pace, coming from the left a man heads my way.

"So now we are going to fuck," he says with a hoarse voice, grabbing me by my cardigan. I try to reason with him, tell him I am having my period, but this only pisses him off and he starts to punch me. It hurts. Not really aiming, my fingers get hold of his cheek. Not holding back, he starts to punch even harder. He stabs me. That's when I knew I wouldn't win this fight. All of a sudden I hear myself scream for help, again and again.

The man loosens his grip and leaves as quickly as he came. I start to run. Seeing a house with the lights on still, I bang on the door. A kind woman asks me in and calls the police. Over the fireplace hangs a mirror. Who is this wounded young woman looking back at me? Her eyebrow cracked open, collarbone bloody with wounds, and a torn cardigan.

The woman also called my boyfriend who seemed to arrive before she'd barely hung up the phone. He took me to the police, to the hospital and…home. Feeling safe, as I lay against his back I can finally sleep.

Although my wounds need time to heal an incomprehensible force pushes me back to work, back to the brothel. I ask my boyfriend to take me by car.

"You don't have to do this, Caroline," he says, not understanding my urge. "But I do," I reply in tears, also not understanding. I get out of the car and rigidly head to the backdoor. The one I've entered so many times before.

A few weeks later I am in the open psychiatric ward. I have had suicidal thoughts since the assault.

What more proof do I need, if even a man in a park thinks he can have his way? I am just not worthy.

During a weekend leave from work, I have a plan… With it, a deep almost joyful calm, took hold of me.

***

The doorbell rings again. I hear a man shout. "We know you are there. This is the police, open up. If not, we will force our way in."

Realizing that there is nothing I can do about it, I reluctantly rise and slowly head for the door. As soon as it opens two uniformed men walk in. One stays with me while the other turns off the gas and opens the kitchen door.

"You are not only putting yourself in danger here, madam," he sounds a bit angry. "This could have caused an explosion not only harming you but many people in the building."

I feel empty. I don't understand why he is making such a fuss. I just want them to leave.

"You are coming with us," the short one says. I can tell they are leading me to the car. No resistance there. I feel no anger. No disappointment. I feel... nothing. I do not care. I am not really there. In slow motion I see the world passing by, as I sit in the backseat. Sounds are muffled, my vision unclear. No input reaches my brain.

"Are you always so apathetic?" My eyes turn to him in silence.

Did someone just ask me something?

At the institution they let me out of the car. I recognize the place, somehow, although the ward I am being brought to is new to me.

"She hasn't spoken one word," they tell the nurse in charge. She looks at me in a way that holds somewhere between pity and sharpness. "Okay, quiet one, you come with me now. I'll show you your room," she says, her encouraging hand kindly on my shoulder. The doors open with a special key. Her shoes click on the sterile beige floor. We stop at a green door.

"You'll spend the night here, Caroline," she says as she un-locks the door.

We enter a cold, empty room. In the middle a bed is covered with white sheets and a yellow blanket. Straps hang loosely on ei-ther side. No table, just one chair.

"Would you like a tea?" I decline with a shake of the head. "Something else maybe, coffee? Water?" Her friendly gesture somehow opens me up a little.

"No thank you." I reply softly, surprised by the sound of my own voice.

"Maybe you just want to go to bed?" She presumes correctly.

The lack of privacy bothers me. During the night, the flashlight of a nurse is lighting my room more than once. I wonder what she is doing. Surely I cannot leave the room without her noticing. Checking to see if I'm still breathing, I suppose. Somehow it feels reassuring. Someone who doesn't know me seems to care. The bed starts to feel comfortable. I fall asleep.

The next morning, I feel different. I bring myself to a sitting position with my legs on the edge of the bed. A thought enters my mind, causing a lightness I have never felt before.

"Now that you're here, Caroline, you might as well make the best of it".

A new calm enters my body.

"Yes, if I can choose to die I can choose to live too," I suddenly realise. I was surprised at how on earth this thought could change my whole being. No, I am not happy. But somehow I still feel, there is another way out.

After breakfast the psychiatrist wants to see me. As I sit at his desk, he hands me a paper. "I kindly ask you to put your signature here, miss. Here at the x. With it you agree to not attempting to take your own life while under our care."

"I can sign, if you want," I replied, "but there is no need. I just realised I am not going to do it anymore. I choose life."

Through the many hours and years of therapy that followed this decision, I started to free myself. Gradually I came to understand that my presence is meaningful. Going back to school I finished not only one, but two courses of study, and even became a therapist for many abused men and women.

I often tell my clients, "We can attend as many schools as we want, but the most important one is called life."

Grateful to be an example of how loving one-self can be learned, I am in love with life. Convinced that everything happens for a reason, taking responsibility and owning my life, I can truly say I am a happy woman. I now know Love is always there, helping us to overcome our traumatic experiences. All we have to do is become aware.

While writing this, I decided to take a break. Needing some other input, I turn on the radio. The second tune I hear is Chaka Khan. I recognize it from the first note and turn up the volume. I dance, feeling happy and grateful, while singing the lyrics I know so well.

"I'm every woman, it's all in me."

About the Author

Caroline Hoek is a transpersonal psychotherapist, coach and trainer. While living in the Netherlands, she considers herself a global citizen and works with clients all over the world.

Caroline is the founder of Good Life Guidance. It is her deepest wish to accompany her clients on the path of personal and/or professional development. Rather than rigid protocols or models, it's her intuition and her 30+ years of experience that are her greatest strengths. Creating a safe, respectful and playful atmosphere, Caroline makes room for what needs to be addressed head on. There's no mannerisms, only guidance for real transformation, letting her clients discover their unique gifts to use for inner and outer leadership. Anchored in (self) trust they no longer go along with the pulls of scarcity or the need to prove themselves.

To learn more, you are invited to download a free e-book or listen to meditations at www.GoodLifeGuidance.com

A Voice From Beyond

Andrea Pennington, MD, C.Ac.

For several years I personally endured dark, bleak and hopeless thoughts about life and my place in it. At various points along my journey the idea of not being on this planet any more seemed like the most reasonable solution to end my emotional pain. Having already tried everything known to me to lift that dark cloud — from antidepressants, talk therapy, exercise, setting and achieving major goals, Shamanic rites of passage and more — my heart ached with deep sadness and a longing for life to be over. I couldn't see any other way out of my pain.

The first time I thought about ending my life I was only a teenager. Filled with the usual adolescent angst and self-doubt, I struggled to find meaning and purpose. At one point the sadness, loneliness and a sense that I didn't belong here were too much to bear. I clearly remember laying on the floor of my bedroom, all alone in the house, staring aimlessly at the loops of carpet beneath me. There was no hint of excitement for life at all, no hope nor optimism of some new experience on the horizon. There was only quiet, still, emptiness and sadness.

My thoughts drifted to how I could end my life without too much mess or pain. I considered pills to be the easiest solution. Tranquilizers like Valium, sleeping pills, and other 'downers' I heard people talk about at school seemed easy to get a hold of. I thought of who I could ask to score some, without arousing suspicion. But as the names and faces of people rolled through my mind I heard a voice gently say, "No. You cannot."

This voice was gentle, quiet and peaceful. It continued, "Andrea you are already pretty aware and conscious, even at your young age. If you kill yourself there is no telling what lower-awareness being you might return as."

I was intrigued. Reincarnation was not something I knew anything about. The voice went on, "If you stick it out in <u>this</u> life, you will get past this pain. You will not suffer forever."

That still, small voice suggested that somehow, someway I *would* get beyond the misery and drudgery I felt life to be. The hint that I might reincarnate as some less conscious being somehow resonated with me, I was scared of suffering even more in the next life. From that point forward I put my fantasies about ending my life to the side — for a time.

Waves of depression and a feeling of despair at the senselessness of life returned during my years at university, but that was after a bad breakup. The words spoken years early still rang in my ears, so I pressed on.

Another bout of depression hit as I made my way through the grueling and intense first two years of medical school. I sought help from our student health system, tried antidepressants for the first time, I was sent to a psychologist, and I was told to play music more often. These interventions did not provide much relief, however. But I wouldn't let myself think about suicide either.

I made it through medical school and my first year of post graduate medical residency with hopes that being in the 'real world' would provide me with meaning, purpose and a break from depression. But depression crept back into my life with an unrelenting persistence.

I thought I was doomed to deal with it for the rest of my life. Having learned that it may be due to a brain chemistry imbalance I tried amino acid mixes, herbs and other supplements. While they helped ease my symptoms from time to time, the mood boost didn't last.

I threw myself into projects, my work, my garden, all in an attempt to ease the burden of darkness. I never would have imagined that the dis-ease that I experienced could have been eradicated if I looked into my own heart and soul for guidance.

Instead I pursued many of the accomplishments, things and experiences that Western society made me believe were equal to happiness. I threw myself into my love relationships. I volunteered at a medical clinic for low income immigrants. I mentored some troubled pre-teens in my neighborhood.

I also built a holistic wellness institute and spa while working as the Medical Director for Discovery Health Channel. While I hosted the news and presented documentaries for the TV network, I worked with an architect to create a space for healing for those who wanted relief from their pain, illness and dysfunction.

Helping other people experience joy again as they tried acupuncture, meditation and group therapy gave me a sense of purpose that lifted the dark cloud of depression. The layout and design of the wellness center was a joy to create from start to finish.

My innate passion for beauty, excellence and compassion were fully engaged, so I felt periods of bliss. I didn't realize that those qualities were aspects of my soul. The highest part of me wanted to be engaged in bringing more light and love to the world. I had no idea that those elements were just as important as exercise and enjoying sun exposure to keep my mental state elevated.

As my medical practice gained recognition with features on TV, including the *Oprah Winfrey Show*, the joy started to slip away. The burden of keeping things going while being on call for my growing TV career prevented me from bringing new energy and insights into the work I did.

Being on TV in the United States sounds like a dream come true to many people. And working for Discovery Communications was indeed a dream of mine. But when I took on the role of Spokesperson for the network, suddenly there were other people dictating how I should look, sound and even what I could and could not say.

Meanwhile I was discovering that I had abilities to 'see' or diagnose disease based on the Traditional Chinese Medicine system, but the conservative media world was skeptical. So much of my emerging interest in bringing to light healing modalities and approaches to wellness that were alternatives to the allopathic medical model was stifled. My nerdy passion for explaining the how and why of healing was put on the back burner.

It wasn't until I spent time with Dr. Martin Seligman while taking a positive psychology coaching program that I discovered that my innate character strengths need to be fully engaged in order for me to feel truly happy. These core strengths and interests needed a place and space to breathe and expand — if not in *all* areas of my life, in enough of them for me to feel whole. My study of positive psychology helped uncover why the depression I felt got worse during times of stress and in response to being silenced from the executives in the TV world.

I came to understand that my drive to be accepted, to not 'rock the boat', to be heard and understood — which began in childhood — made me compromise on my truth. Way back in my teenage years as I started to explore personal development, psychology and mysticism, I felt a tug and a pull to learn more. It was thrilling. Then, reaching adulthood and finding that many Eastern cultures allowed for free discussion and exploration of the mind-body-spirit connection led to extreme frustration. I wanted to share and feel ALL of what life has to offer and that was not possible with the work life I was in.

My training along with my real world experience were pointing the way to my salvation: I needed to integrate my whole being — mind-body-soul — with my whole life. It was not good enough for me to explore spirituality on the sidelines while appearing on TV and stages across America sharing only half-truths. I needed to utilize my talents, live in accordance with my soul's deepest desires and interact with others in alignment with my core values.

Despite the success and fame my career afforded me, it was not fulfilling on the most important levels. And I wasn't the only one who felt this way. I could see this same pattern of self-denial and self-hatred in my clients. While my lack of self-love was experienced as depression and anxiety, other people felt intense urges which led to addictive behavior or eating disorders. Some of my clients saw their bodies react with illness, infection and autoimmune conditions the more they silenced themselves.

Not sharing our truth and not living in alignment with our values can lead to a soul-ache, a sense of worthlessness in life. It is only now being recognized that following the advice of society, religion and our families can lead us into careers, marriages and lifestyles that slowly kill our sense of purpose and drive for life. And when we feel life is bleak or burdensome, many people seek relief in food, relationships, drugs, gambling, shopping or hiding under the blankets while streaming shows online.

The challenge for me, and so many of my patients, was that we felt there was no way out. We felt trapped. And that's when dark depressive and even suicidal thoughts can creep in and overwhelm us. When we cannot see a way out of our pain or beyond the situations that are draining our life force it is easy to understand why suicide seems like the best option.

In 2005 I hit a serious low and I wanted out of life again. At the end of the summer I found a mini-escape while on vacation in Spain and France. The real deliverance from my depression was to come through a spiritual awakening that happened after a glorious night of expressing my soul's desire to sing, emote and be seen as I really am. I have described that momentous spiritual experience on the French Riviera elsewhere[1], which included a cracking open of my heart through total despair that provided a miraculous lifting of the dark veil of depression. I had an out of body connection in a near death like experience where I was merged with a loving energy that I experienced as *Oneness*.

In a matter of moments I realized that my whole life had been leading me to one major realization, something that our spirit knows all along: in order to enjoy a life of total wellness and happiness on earth we must become and express who we *really* are — not who our parents, society, or religion force us to be. None of our past programming, life experience, or trauma totally dictates or limits who we are or who we can become.

The understanding of these principles was instantaneous and certain. I felt with complete assuredness that to live a life of freedom and joy, we can align our actions with our spirit, rather than the ego or programs of the soul. As I explained in my TEDx, to do so we must *learn* who we *really* are, *love* who we are and *live* who we are. We are creators of life, including our own.

During that experience I realized that I'm not wrong, bad, or selfish for wanting to feel like I matter and for wanting to be seen for who I really am.

---

[1] I have shared how in a fit of despair and depression I called on God to my life, which led to a near death-like experience that removed depression from me. To learn more, visit YouTube to see my TEDx "Become Who You Really Are" and read my story in the book *Magic & Miracles*.

In the peaceful presence of Oneness all my previous programming and biases were replaced and I saw a vision of myself living joyfully on the French Riviera. In this radiant vision of new life I was holding hands with a child walking near the beach, I was singing professionally and I could heal people with my hands. Though stunned by the bizarreness of this life vision, I was inspired. In fact, I felt a total acceptance to return to my life, but with renewed enthusiasm to live according to my deepest desires. I said, "Yes" to Life and a few days later I returned to America a changed woman. There was no returning to the inauthentic version of me!

It took some time to cut the ties with my former way of life and as I did I started an intensive meditation, yoga, and QiGong practice. I eventually moved to France, my young daughter holding my hand. Through deep introspection and living from my strengths, passions, dreams, and desires I now feel confident in who I am. Anchored in my Truth I have consciously constructed my life and career *on my terms*. I now truly love myself and enjoy greater well-being than I thought possible!

I don't think you need to move to a foreign country, perform onstage, or have an out-of-body near-death-like experience to learn — or remember — that you are totally lovable and acceptable as you are. My path was quite a convoluted adventure to total wellness and personal fulfillment. I've since discovered that by following a few simple steps, you can return to knowing your authentic self, it's like returning to your true home.

I now work with the sole intention of helping other people break free from the mental anguish and suffering that being so far away from your Authentic Self causes. In addition to openly sharing my story in my first TEDx and in my book, *I Love You, Me!*, I offer online mentoring, guidance and connection through the Real Self Love Movement. If this resonates with you at all I invite you to join our beautiful community of sharing and sup-port. It is offered free for all who wish to join.

Details are at www.RealSelf.love

Wishing you all the love your heart can hold, and then some,

Andrea

2
Recovering from Relationship Trauma

I t is not at all uncommon to hear from survivors of traumatic relationships that their experiences of relationship struggles began in childhood. Typically, the way we interact with our parents becomes a blueprint for our future relationships. We learn to think and behave like those who influence us when we are young and impressionable.

From the world of neuroscience and developmental psychology comes a wealth of information on how this occurs at the cellular level. Before the age of seven, our brains are sponge-like and form the neural pathways that see us into adulthood, all the way to old age, where of course these pathways begin to wither. This is why the lessons that we learn in childhood stay with us so strongly; the good, the bad, and everything in between.

Of course, as impressionable children, nearly everything we pick up from an influential adult may be taken onboard as a 'truth' – whether it's a universal truth or or just their opinionated version of truth. This often encompasses our parents' beliefs, preferences, religion, and lessons from their own upbringings. Our sense of self-worth and what we are capable of experiencing in life is also partially developed in response to our upbringing.

The relationship we have with ourselves is crucial to our happiness. When you look at how you relate to yourself, how much or little you allow yourself to follow your dreams, it's a good indicator of how much unhappiness you are willing to accept. This is very often mirrored in our relationships with others too.

When we have learned to make room for the desires of others to the detriment of our own happiness, fulfillment and room to grow, you can be sure that is the biggest red flag you will ever have waved for you.

Yet how often do we turn our gaze away from that red flag? How often do we tell ourselves to be patient, be forgiving, and that maybe we deserved the mistreatment we have experienced?

The brave souls in Part 3 have all learned to move past that way of thinking. They questioned the 'truths' they learned in childhood, and found their way out the other side. They stand now more empowered, conscious and resilient. Their stories prove this in beautiful ways.

Many people who experience relationship trauma in childhood or early adolescence have gone on to find themselves in similarly difficult relationships as adults; a growing number of survivors are now breaking out of that pattern. As survivors support each other and start to feel more brave, many more people are telling their stories. These stories show other survivors that they are not alone, and even inspire them to find their own way out of unhappiness to begin again.

If you or someone you care about is in a difficult situation right now, then please know that there are more of us survivors out here, and we all want you to find your own freedom. I hope that the following real life stories give you strength and inspire you to believe that there is a happy life after relationship trauma waiting for you.

Breaking Free from a Narcissist

Funmi Moser, MD

Iwas in a 7-year relationship with a narcissist and I didn't have a clue…

It wasn't until all of my attention was focused on our newborn son, who needed medical care, that the relationship fell apart. I will never forget the night before my 9-month-old son's operation. I took a walk on a bridge across a river that was near the hospital because we both couldn't sleep. I was carrying him in a carrier on my chest and I remember looking down into the water and thinking if I were to jump, we would be both gone and lost; perishing before anyone could find us.

Yes, I had suicidal thoughts that night. I was in a relationship, yet I felt so alone and deserted. I didn't kill myself or drown my child that night, or I wouldn't be here to share my story.

The story actually started a long time ago, when I had finished my medical studies and gotten my first job in the neuroradiology department of a university hospital in Germany.

It was there I met the future father of my son. He was charming, larger than life and a breath of fresh air. He was an anestheisologies who came to sedate the children before we could examine them in our scanners. I found it fascinating how fast and effortless he could put the children to sleep. They never cried for long and I thought, "Oh, such a nice loving doctor, who loves children…". I searched for and caught his attention and we started dating.

He had another girlfriend at the time, but I didn't know it. There were so many signs of trouble at the beginning of the relationship that I chose to ignore. Although he was a doctor and earned enough money, he chose to live in a one room apartment. A messy apartment. He hoarded magazines which were strewn everywhere. He had two cars and a motorbike. He also had twins, who lived with their mother in France and whom he hardly visited. His relationship with his mother was not healthy either, and he hardly had any real friends.

Some years into the relationship, I noticed that his sexual drive and fantasies were very strange and not aligned to mine. When he refused to move into a flat we could share, I knew he was reluctant to commit more to the relationship. So after a year, when I got the opportunity to work in Switzerland, I took it and we had a long-distance relationship for several years, which suited him but was very unsatisfactory for me.

I wanted him to look for a job also in Switzerland but he never seriously looked. He eventually got a good paying job in Luxembourg but was living again in a room in the nursing home of the hospital.

Then I found out I was expecting! It came as a shock to us and at his request, I aborted. A decision I regret to this day.

We remained together even after that trauma. Eventually, I asked that we move to the same city and live together. By this time we had been a couple for four years. Two years later, I wanted a child again and I shared my wish with him. Eventually we were expecting. I was happy of course, but he wasn't.

This time, I refused to discuss another abortion and said I would take full responsibility of the child on my own. My determination was challenged when I discovered our child needed medical care and several operations, too. It was very scary for me and going through it alone all the more difficult. Shortly after his first operation, I got him into daycare so that I could go back to work. I wanted to take my final examinations to become a radiology consultant, but I underestimated how much I had to study for the exam and so was not well prepared.

Despite fulfilling the examination board's six-month, full-time work requirement and also working part-time, I failed my examination and had to retake it. But once I passed and things settled down, I found that I enjoyed going back to work. I tried to manage child, work and house responsibilities on my own. It was tough, but I coped.

Around this time, my boyfriend started being openly unfaithful and I couldn't take it anymore. I say openly because looking back there were signs and proof that he'd always been unfaithful to me. It was the last straw in a very dramatic and challenging year and a half of taking care of my son alone in a so-called relationship.

With the help of my family, I found a place for myself and moved out. Three months later the woman he'd been cheating with while still with me dumped him, so he got desperate and wanted to come back. He was depressed and had suicidal thoughts, but it was all based in selfishness. I didn't need that. After all, I was slowly getting back my self-confidence and self-worth.

During that time, my sister recommended two books to me, one called *The Journey from Abandonment to Healing* by Susan Anderson, and the other, *Feel the Fear and Do It Anyway* by Susan Jeffers. The first book helped me to get over the loss of the relationship, how to recognize the different stages and how to plow through. The second book helped me to feel free to dream again and to follow my dreams even if I was terrified.

My ex kept stalking me. Sometimes I'd see his car in my neighborhood and I'd receive upsetting calls from him. I didn't feel safe in my new home and felt haunted every time I stepped out of the house.

He became aggressive claiming I had not helped him out when he needed me, as if I could protect him from his suicidal thoughts. I didn't discount his issues, but what could I do? I was out of the country at the time visiting my sister so I advised him to seek professional help. I knew he had a psychiatrist friend and suggested he talk to him, but he didn't listen to me. He wanted me to save him. I couldn't.

He even called my mom and told her he was thinking of killing himself. She quickly got professional advice from a psychologist and called him back to ask him if he was serious. She told him she would have to call the police to prevent him from causing harm to himself. He promptly said it was only a thought and he wasn't going to act upon it. This was all very distressing for me and I didn't know how to handle the situation.

The turning point was when a friend of mine mentioned that maybe I had been codependent in a toxic relationship. That's when I started studying the psychology behind that.

Being codependent in a relationship means that you condone bad behavior from your partner and you find reasons to defend the person. You live in denial of your reality and are isolated. This codependence is mostly seen in relationships where one person is an alcoholic. My ex wasn't an alcoholic, so I kept researching.

I discovered that codependence is also found in relationships with narcissists. If you also have a helper syndrome, you are more likely to be attractive for a narcissist. Then I started studying what narcissism is. That is when I found out that I had been in a relationship with a covert narcissist (i.e., a narcissist who masks their true self through an outwardly charming demeanor). That explained a lot.

So, who is a narcissist? I will try as best as I can to explain.

It is not an easy thing to pinpoint. There are people who have only certain traits of narcissism in them but do not fulfill the diagnosis of a narcissistic personality disorder (NPD). The common characteristics are their lack of empathy and a personal disdain for other people; persistent grandiosity and an excessive need for admiration.

To satisfy their needs, they seek to establish abusive power and control over others. They value themselves over others to the extent that they openly disregard the feelings and wishes of others, and expect to be treated as superior, regardless of their actual status or achievements. They often have a fragile ego, are intolerant of criticism and tend to belittle others in order to validate their own superiority.

Narcissistic personality disorder usually develops in adolescence or during early adulthood. The cause is not really known but some think it begins in childhood, when a defenseless child is not loved by a parent. The parent might be a narcissist themselves and lacks the ability to love. The neglected child builds defenses around him or herself allowing no one to get close so that they are not hurt by possible rejection. The child never learns what true unconditional love is, or how to love oneself and others. They grow up only being concerned with themselves and their feelings. They feel a constant void and lack in their lives and try to fill that up. They have narcissistic cravings, as described in the Diagnostic and Statistical Manual of Mental Disorders.

True symptoms of NPD are pervasive, apparent in varied situations, and rigid, remaining consistent over time. NPD symptoms must be sufficiently severe to significantly impair the person's capabilities to develop meaningful human relationships.

Getting back to my ex. I am not trying to say that he has NPD, but he has exhibited many of the traits and it just helped me to understand and deal with him accordingly. He also had a manic-depressive condition that is common among narcissists. So during the periods he felt unloved, he was depressed and stalked me. All this time he never showed any interest in our son. It wasn't until I demanded child-support from him that he got angry again and then started demanding to see our son. Around this time, he got into another relationship and left me alone for a while... until the next break-up.

Understanding his narcissistic nature helped me to cope with his manic-depressive behavior and most importantly I learned to create boundaries for myself and my child. On my journey of healing, I grew stronger and found my old self again. I was taking good care of myself and my son.

I soon started preparing for my examination to become a radiologist. Around this time a friend of mine talked to me about the law of attraction and the short documentary called "The Secret". I found all I could online and in books and started educating myself on the subject of the movie, the Law of Attraction. I wanted to reprogram my subconscious to manifest the things I wanted to have in my life. So with positive affirmations every day and of course good preparation, I passed my exams.

The next thing I tackled was asking myself what kind of man I wanted in my life. I knew I had to break the cycle I had in the past of getting into toxic relationships. So, I started working on myself.

I wrote a list of all the qualities I needed in the character of my future partner. While still in the process, I started dating and eventually found someone who was the perfect fit. Things have been going really well for us. In fact, we have just welcomed our first child together.

Of course, I am still a work in progress. I still have to maintain boundaries with my ex. I have to guide and help my son to deal with his father when he is with him. It's not easy and there are times when I am frustrated. The problem with narcissists is that they feel they are right all the time, they lack empathy for others and do not change. As a result, the underlying problems remain the same, the difference is I am conscious of them and deal with them as best as I can.

I am sharing my story in order to reach out to others who may be in a similar situation. I am so grateful for all the help I received from friends, family and self-help books that I would like to give back.

Everyone has a different voice and maybe with mine I can reach out to a certain audience that will feel some resonance with my story and be helped or at least directed towards help.

This is just to say you are not alone in your struggles, you are not crazy, there is an explanation for the toxic relationship you experienced or are experiencing. I'm here to encourage you along your pathway to dealing with it.

Being a single mom has enough challenges as it is, so dealing with those challenges and the added complexity of dealing with a narcissist is a big deal.

As long as one has to keep in contact for the child's sake it is also a situation that one has to deal with for a very long time. Some books say it is best to cut off all contact with a narcissist. I agree. It would be easier, but unfortunately it's not applicable in my situation. So I now know that I must exercise endurance and keep working on myself — as all of us should — to be an expression of my best self in this world.

References:

"Feel the Fear and Do It Anyway" by Susan Jeffers

"The Journey from Abandonment to Healing" by Susan Anderson

"Narzissmus: Das innere Gefängnis" by Heinz-Peter Röhr

"The Diagnostic and Statistical Manual of Mental Disorders(DSM–5)" by the American Psychiatric Association

About the Author

My name is Dr. Funmi Moser, born to a German mother and Nigerian father. We moved to Nigeria and later I came back to Germany to study medicine. I trained to become a radiologist in Germany and Switzerland. I am a single mom of my 6 year old son. I live and work in Germany.

If you'd like support you may contact me at angela77moser@gmail.com

From Darkness to Light

The Keys to a Free & Empowered life

Marike Stassar

The Event That Changed My Life

Imagine that one friend who seems to live the perfect life. She is happy, beautiful, full of energy and ideas, good at music and sports. She excels at school, comes from a loving family and boys easily fall in love with her. Whatever she lays her hands on seems to work out. Do you know anyone like that? This is what the first 18 years of my life looked like.

I had a blissful childhood and rolled through my schooldays without much struggle. I was hard working and gave my very best to everything I did. I loved life! I remember thinking to myself, "I can do whatever I want!" I always saw the best in others, too; I didn't think that people would ever do any harm to each other. Some call that attitude naïve, some call it pure. I didn't think much of it at the time. It was simply the way I saw the world.

Then I turned 18 and finished my high school exams. I couldn't wait to fly away from my parent's nest, live on my own and study in the big city. I was so looking forward to being able to do whatever I felt like, eat as many cookies as I wanted and stay up late. But first up was a summer holiday in Mallorca with a friend to celebrate finishing school. It was my first holiday without my parents.

What a joy! I warmed my body in the Spanish sun, ate food with exotic names and danced until my feet hurt. Then one night this nice local guy started dancing with me. It made me feel like I was in heaven! But my heaven soon turned into hell. I didn't notice that he kept feeding me drinks, more than I was used to. Soon after, I was drunk and couldn't find my friend anymore. I was put into a car and driven to a stranger's house where I was repeatedly raped. My world fell apart. I couldn't understand how anyone could hurt someone else like that.

That night I lost my purity and my virginity. And I was yet to find out how severely this one event would impact the rest of my life.

The First Signs Of Emotional Damage

Once home, I broke up with my boyfriend without mentioning why. I didn't tell anyone what had happened. I was ashamed and felt like a bird with a broken wing. I had the courage to get the physical damage treated, but the emotional scars were left to heal by themselves. I simply wanted to forget the whole thing and put it behind me. As planned, I moved out of my parent's home and started my university studies.

Life seemed to normalize. I did very well at school and enjoyed student life. Boys fell in love with me like before, but something had changed, I had become very jealous in relationships and immediately thought of suicide when I sensed my boyfriend might leave me. I didn't understand myself and couldn't control my thoughts and feelings. I saw it as simply how I was and that there was nothing I could do about it.

I didn't know then that things would go from bad to worse the longer I denied what was happening to me. It took me 30 years to be able to connect the dots and understand that my destructive behavior was a natural reaction to what had happened to me in Mallorca.

The Good, Bad And Ugly Consequences

Years went by, during which I was unknowingly driven by desperation to feel loved and special. I broke up my marriage and stopped my PhD project after three years because I felt unappreciated for who I was. I became harsher with my opinions and behavior, did well in the corporate world, got promoted several times and felt proud of myself. At work I felt strong – no one could touch me – and I wore my smiling mask most of the time.

But inside the four walls of my own home, I experienced the opposite side of that coin. I often felt sad, misunderstood and afraid of not being loved. I reacted to the slightest form of criticism with defense and anger and had become a master at pointing out others' mistakes. Later, I understood that this was my way of coping with my own low self-worth.

I got married again and became the mother of two beautiful boys. Motherhood sparked the soft and loving side that I had buried deep inside me. As a consequence, my marriage soon started colliding with what was going on inside of me. I wanted to be more positive and loving, but I simply did not know how. I was constantly triggered into showing the worst side of myself. It was like wearing this big red button that was pushed at the slightest touch, setting off a chain reaction of anger, frustration, and sadness.

It devastated me, especially in front of my kids. Feeling like a bad mother added to my sadness and confusion. But a divorce and jumping into a new relationship were the only ways that I knew how to feel loved again. So that is exactly what I did.

Hitting Rock Bottom

At first, this new relationship was all I was living for. It gave me exactly what I needed to feel loved, beautiful and special. But as soon as the pink cloud drifted away, the summer of love turned into a chilly autumn that was followed by a cold and dark winter and I felt more trapped with my emotions than ever before. Whenever I showed any sign of anger or frustration, I saw my worst dream come true, he left me. We would come back together a few days later, only to repeat the same cycle again. And again. I felt totally frustrated and helpless.

To avoid these constant break-ups, I started to behave like I was expected to. I desperately tried to keep all the unwanted emotions inside, thereby allowing myself to be driven further and further away from who I really was. I was walking on eggshells.

I sank into a deep depression and cried every day. When I got up in the morning, I was often tired and didn't know how to make it through the day. I was struggling for my own survival, while trying to keep all the balls of everyday life in the air: two small children, a household and a full-time job. I lived in a country that wasn't my own and I missed my family. I felt lonely and misunderstood.

I started knocking on several doors of the traditional health system, but no one could really help me. During my darkest moment of depression, my body finally gave up. I literally couldn't move anymore. I understood I needed serious help and checked into a psychiatric hospital.

Light in the Darkness

And then one day, a few months later, while I was in the shower trying to let the hot water wash the sadness from my face,

I had a vision. I saw a man with a small beard dressed in white robes standing in front of me. He looked at me with kind eyes and handed me a golden key. And I heard a voice inside me say, "This is the key to your heart." Even though I didn't know what it meant, it immediately gave me comfort. I stopped crying, got out of the shower and went on with my day without giving the experience another thought.

A few months later during the summer holidays, I unexpectedly got a few extra days to myself when my kids went to visit their family. A good friend suggested I join her in Denmark for healing and relaxation with a spiritual teacher she respected. Something in me said yes.

And there he was standing in front of me in Denmark, the man from my vision in person! As soon as he saw me, he gave the kindest smile of recognition like he was meeting a long-lost friend. It immediately melted all the doubts I had about this trip. I didn't need to tell him my story, he simply understood what I was going through and gave me the tools and insights I needed to heal my wounds.

His words, "Don't WANT love; you ARE love!" still ring in my ears. But I had no clue how to BE love! I still desperately WANTED to be loved, accepted and feel special as a result of others' actions. However, I had also come to understand that this was what had caused all my troubles in the first place.

I was more than willing to invite the spiritual teacher's different and somewhat strange kind of help into my life and started to attend his workshops and healings on a regular basis. He taught me how to meditate and I awakened to the truth of who I really am. Slowly but surely, I saw myself and the world around in a more positive way.

Emotional Self-Healing Process

My depressive episodes didn't immediately go away, but I had a better grip on them. I still had mornings when I got out of bed feeling tired, depressed and sad, but I did my meditation anyway and felt relief and control. This became my regular way of life and after a while, I had a major breakthrough.

Suddenly while meditating on the third day of a new depressive episode, I felt something open up on the top of my head, which let a flow of feel-good energy pour into my body. And the depressive feeling instantly disappeared! Then I understood that when we are in a state of depression we close ourselves off from a significant part of our life energy. Meditation reconnects us, letting the energy flow in again, which makes the depression disappear. This turned out to be a significant step in my process of emotional self-healing.

Soon my life took a turn in a much better direction than I could ever have imagined. I gained the strength to end the destructive relationship I was in. My work life flourished and I connected well with my children again. I was finally able to look forward to each day and enjoy life as it presented itself.

The Dawn of Happiness

During the time that followed, I learned a lot about myself and how life operates. I started noticing synchronicities that seemed to help me so that when I lost my job a few years later, I could see the opportunity that was carefully wrapped up inside this experience to help me find my next direction in life.

I used the time at home to reflect and discover what I really wanted to do. I realized that over the course of my life I had gathered all these tools that helped me heal from trauma. They are like beautiful jewels waiting to be shared with others who are also searching for a way out of their difficult situation. I immediately recognized that this is what I was meant to do.

To become even more equipped to help people where other systems have failed, I invested in as many courses and education as I could. I quit my well-paid job and started working as an transformational coach using a method I had discovered from my own life. And I'd like to share it with you.

The Free & Empowered Method – 3 steps to a joyful life after trauma

These three steps are what will heal your trauma and help you start living a joyful & purposeful life:

1. Free yourself
2. Empower yourself
3. Be yourself

1. <u>Free yourself</u> means to understand what, how and why you think, speak, act and feel the way you do, and how to break free from it.

After going through a trauma, you unknowingly lose a part of yourself. This can be your self-worth or sense of security, belonging or trust. Most people unconsciously try to compensate for that loss by looking for something outside of themselves. This can be love (unhealthy relationship) or work (workaholic), as well as alcohol and drugs. In my case, I had lost my self-worth and needed to feel loved by being in a relationship to make up for that — even if that meant I had to become a different person and be miserable to keep that relationship.

But there comes a time when you are ready to let all of that go and become the better and authentic version of yourself again. Realizing and changing what you have lost and how you have compensated for that loss is a process that is best done with the help of a life coach, for example, so you can really transform your traumatic experiences.

2. Empower yourself means loving yourself as you are, with all your beautiful imperfections, at a physical, emotional and spiritual level.

From experience I know that this can be a difficult step – especially after a sex, love or relationship trauma. But there are several tools to help you!

Putting a hand on your heart and breathing slowly while keeping your focus on your heart area for a few minutes every day can help you connect back with the love inside you. Remember: you ARE love! Also, trust whatever is coming your way. It is there to help you, even if it doesn't look anything like help.

3. Be yourself means rediscovering who you are and what you really want in life.

Here is where true happiness lies, to live a life that is aligned with who you really are and doing what you are really passionate about.

I believe that everyone has a purpose and gift that is waiting to be shared. There are tools and techniques to tap into your greater Power, discover your true passion and live life from your highest potential.

I am the living example that it is possible to obtain this.

And if I can do it, YOU CAN DO IT!

About the Author

Hi, my name is Marike Stassar. I'm from the Netherlands and currently live in the heart of Oslo, Norway. I am a passionate transformational coach and empowerment teacher. I am on a mission to help people like you and me move past trauma, reconnect with who you really are and find your gift in life. Based on my personal experiences, I designed the three-step Free & Empowered method that gives you the tools and insights to move past your trauma, get empowered and live a happy and purposeful life.

I believe that everyone deserves the life they truly desire, and I would like nothing more than to help you achieve exactly that!

I'd love to connect with you. Please send me an email, follow me on Facebook and Instagram and visit my website:

contact@marikestassar.com
facebook.com/marikestassar
instagram.com/marikestassar
marikestassar.com

The Journey to Find My True Self

Anna Frostin

I got a serious illness 1986 and the doctors did not give me much hope. I had a near death experience which was the start for me to challenge my Mom's negative judgment about me. Six years later my brother got cancer at only only 48 years old. His last two months of life opened up more understanding and love for him, myself and others. From my diary I share with you all these difficulties memories.

To My Brother

The warm sun is shining as the wind slowly plays in your curls. Bumble-bees are humming, a little yellow butterfly flashes in the wind, and the sea-waves accompany with their powerful sound. I look with tenderness and love at your face. How could all this happen?

With your entry into this world, my parents got what they had been longing for — a son. You became a successful professor and received such attention and appreciation. Now suddenly everything changed when you suffer from a life-threatening cancer and your wife chooses divorce because she doesn't love you.

In May, I visit you at Lund's University Hospital, where I discover major shortcomings in our amazing healthcare. You are lying in your bed, unreachable. You don't get any help. When I read your fluid balance record in your medical chart, it shows that you lost much more fluid than you received. Your state of health is life-threatening.

With the list in my hand I walk out to discuss your case with the responsible doctor, who acts quickly. Within 15 minutes you receive two bottles of nutritional solutions; a shot in each arm. Your condition changes quickly and you become clear-headed. My joy is great when that evening, we go for a walk in the hospital park.

My own work situation is very pressured because I have started a pioneering job at the Karolinska Institute in Stockholm. They want to begin a new form of therapy and the task is given to me, which requires that I travel to the United States and England to study. Back in 1992 Cognitive Behavioral Therapy (CBT) was an unknown therapy, which quickly became popular. Soon many doctors and psychologists from different parts of Sweden wanted to attend my courses. Because I also have many other psychotherapy courses to teach my work situation is really tough.

Per, you will not have to stay in the hospital. We will make it possible for you to stay in your house, which you have built with your own hands. My husband, who is a physician, and I want to take care of your nursing care and treatment. Your difficult pain requires high doses of morphine. The strange thing is that when I am working with you, you become pain free. Can hands heal? It takes many hours every day, which brings me into contact with the tapestry of difficult memories from our childhood and all the pain I had tried to hide.

Unwanted From Birth

When I was born, it was a big disappointment because our mother longed for a son. And when you were born, her dream was fulfilled. To the family, you were the important one. I was left with my aunt at the age of two; a sensitive time for a child. After two and a half months it was time to come home. In my aunt's diary we can read that on the way home they had packed all their belongings in a taxi, but after a few kilometers they discovered that I'm not in the car, I was left in the locked house.

You were always our mom's darling and her super intelligent son and I was judged to be the opposite. A child lives up to the environment's expectations. And Mother's view is wrong. No one tried to understand the reason for me having less strength than other children. I was not stupid, but my psychical health was a problem. Being both physically and mentally abandoned can create a deep impression on a child.

At six years old, I suffered from low body temperature for six months. My temperature was below 36°C and our parents did not search for medical help. A few years later, the school doctor discovered two serious heart failures, which put me in the hospital, where I was bedridden for nine months. I longed to go home and celebrate Christmas so the doctor gave me permission to leave for Christmas Eve and Christmas Day. But on Christmas Eve I wanted to return to the hospital because the loneliness there was not as apparent as at home.

Since I had to spend nine months in the hospital I lost a whole school year. You were promoted so then we were in the same classroom. For me it was hard to do the same things as the other children and therefore I was left alone during every school break. But you, you were the star in the class. Not being important to anyone made me feel terrible, and it went on for seven years.

It was hard for me to breathe because of my heart problems and this caused me anxiety. How often did I stand alone with my anxiety and knock on our mother's door that remained locked? I tried to make myself invisible to reduce my pain and shame. When Mom was angry she shouted, "I regret that I birthed you." It was therefore better for me to say nothing. Mom and Donald

Trump have skills to convince people: to be angry and to be hurt are ways to get control and benefit from others.

To talk about caring creates a longing, but being constantly betrayed makes the big black hole of sadness bigger. Do they see and still not care? To my entire family I was invisible. Why? No dialogue? No one saw me. No one talked about it, not even my teachers. Instead of denying it they could have tried to understand my situation. My life could have changed quickly if they sent me to a new school. A new environment could probably have changed my life.

As a twelve-year-old boy, by your writings in newspapers against female priests you got the media's attention. The years passed and mother's vision of me did not change "there will never be anything of you." I have many written letters with these negative judgments from her.

What can a 16-year-old girl do? I decided to trust myself and move from our home and rent a 6m² room and start to earn my own money. I am alone and want to change my life; not an easy task. From 17-years-old onward I have provided my own living with no financial contribution from my parents nor from society.

Finding New Hope

I happen to win some beauty contests and they offered me exciting work as a travelling model. I got work in Paris, Rome, Athens and London. Cool! My joy was great. But our parents considered my job superficial and sinful. Even if I wasn't living at home, I must, like a child, get my parents' approval. They said no. My dad asked my sister for help to convince me to end this unflattering career.

On a modeling job, I meet one of Sweden's greatest entertainers, Povel Ramel. The first time he sees me he opens his arms and says, "Oh, how beautiful you are."

"Does he mean me?" The thought sticks in my head. These are words had I never heard from my family.

You can oppose your parents' opinions but when these mix with the rules from the Bible, it awakens feelings of guilt. I wanted to be good and do the right thing, so with sadness in my heart, I said no to jobs as a photo and runway model and took a job as a cleaner in a hospital. No one in the family seemed to think it wasn't I job for me. After half a year, a stranger recognized my talents and after two hours, I got a new job and started my medical education.

What happened in your life, Per? Your study performance got attention from the media, and the newspapers paid attention when you became the youngest priest in Sweden, at only 20 years old. And you also spent a year serving in the military.

The family sees your accomplishment and they are proud. But who in the family sees me? It's not easy to both study and work. But after five years of studying anatomy, physiology and pathology, I earn a teacher's competence. One of the world's largest pharmaceutical companies recruits me. My responsibility involves clinical trials, workshops for doctors and marketing.

What Is Love?

Per, what is love? Many think that passion is the same as love. What happens when we meet the great love? Shall we not receive that love with open arms?

What happened to you and what happened to me? You chose a person who is the opposite of our mother. I met many men in my life who said that they love me, but all those who have not learned to love themselves can easily go wrong. For me it was nine years that ended in disaster. I became pregnant and the experience of having a person growing day by day within me was magic. But my husband said, "I do not want a child and you have to abort." *"Never!"* I thought. But my stress was high and resulted in a miscarriage.

While we were building our longed-for home and doing the work ourselves, I received a phone call from my boss. He told me that the three employees should be fired. After the call I returned to the work I was doing with a large cleavage saw. Suddenly the saw hit me. The muscles from three fingers on my left hand were peeled off.

A good hand surgeon saved my hand, but for several months, the risk of bleeding is high. As I was recovering my husband traveled on business trips to other countries and fell in love with a woman from another country. She conceived his child. With no money, I am forced to live all summer in a tent.

Although I was suffering in that crisis, our dad and our sister made a long trip to Africa to visit you, Per. Our father was a good person and a wonderful priest. Our family wanted to be good Christian people and so they worked to help others. But what is "goodness"? Is it true that doing good things for others makes one a good person?

The Tide Turns

I had a serious rheumatic disease and needed to take antibiotics every time I got an infection, otherwise it could damage my heart. After many years of taking antibiotics my body stopped responding to them. The doctors gave me high doses of cortisone and cytostatic to prevent cell growth but it did not help much.

My intuition told me to find other ways to build up my health in a natural way so I booked a cheap airplane ticket from cold Sweden to the other side of the globe.

A new man came into my life and he asked me to marry him. He trusts the medical approach and chooses to take care of his patients instead of joining the trip. What happens next is completely magical when I meet people who change my world. Instead of a hotel, I find a safe place to stay every day. I have a transforming meeting in the mountains where a guru looks at me with his loving eyes and asks "What's missing in your life, just now"? Such an important question! In the NOW we have everything.

Two Months To Live

Per, before your death you had two important months where we both come into contact with our true self and love. These months are really important for both of us. We had many talks and time in silence, experiencing closeness to our true selves. We had a vital dialogue between "I" and "You". We touched deeply what it means to be yourself and you opened up for love. What you have given will go on in your three lovely children.

***

It was a summer day when Per was buried. From different parts of the world more than 500 people gathered in the great Cathedral of Lund to say goodbye, which shows how important he was important to many people.

My husband and I remained there more than a month, but having just bought a new house, we looked forward to getting back home to unpack. But that was not to be. We arrived home to find a broken window and all our boxes strewn across the lawn. Empty. All our valuables gone.

Putting the Pieces Together

How can we solve a problem if we don't understand the problem? What happens if the solution is a part of the problem?

My lack of self-esteem forced me to compensate so I tried to be perfect. I always sought knowledge from the best professors in my field and they helped me to become a pioneer in the construction work of CBT in Sweden, which has now been the most important therapy in Swedish healthcare. But too much work and stress and not taking care of my health led to two very serious diseases, including PTSD.

I had a near-death experience that changed my view of life. Plus, my meeting with Jon Kabat-Zinn, the Dalai lama and Nelson Mandela helped me in seeking my inner core; all powerful journeys.

Why do we not want to see the most obvious? This is a problem both in my family unit and in the bigger world. We live with stress in a fragmented world and continue in our old tracks, without questioning if it's the right way.

My 35 years of working with clients in psychotherapy has taught me a lot. My parents had a strong will to be good Christian people and they did many good things for others but failed to see what was happening in their own family.

What happens when rules are more important than life itself? Rigid rules can prevent us from becoming our true selves. What good are rules that demand that we strive for success and become consumed by that pursuit? Will it bring happiness or will it end with "emptiness" and more consuming?

What about people with different religions whose rules seem strange to us? What happens if we do not try to understand our own and others beliefs?

Is not the source of our most important religions the same? It is love. Only the rules of each religion are different. I have come to understand that dialogue can help us grow closer to each other and lead to a better understanding.

'NOW' Is Full of Joy

My life is a miracle. Because I have health-problems, I need to work harder to take care of my body. I train to build my strength, eat healthy food, do yoga, dance and walk in the mountains. I am now grateful for my many amazing friends, our quality-time and laughter together. My life is an exciting adventure.

What has my life experience taught me? *Goodness comes from the heart* not from the head and not from judging. Replace grasping for happiness with ease, acceptance and being in the NOW.

About the Author

Hi, I am Anna Frostin, an accredited psychotherapist in Sweden. I have worked more than thirty years to help clients to change dysfunctional thoughts, feelings, behaviors, rules and core beliefs.

My first book was about Cognitive Behavioral Therapy (CBT) for physicians. I have worked for Karolinska Institute in Stockholm and have had taught courses and lectures in CBT and Mindfulness and have now workshops for different groups. My second book is about how to reduce negative stress, sleep problems, anxiety and depression.

Now am I working with a new book and groups for helping people to understand the difference between naïveté and real goodness from our heart. My goal is to help people to better use their strengths for developing both goodness for ourselves and the world. I believe that the most important thing is to understand "who you are".

Connect with Anna:
www.kognitivterapi.se
psychotherapist.annaf@gmail.com
info@kognitivterapi.se

Diving Deep Into the Depths of My World

Karin Eke

'The cure for the pain is in the pain' ~ Rumi

I grew up with a perfectly inexistent existence. Truly, I was not seen, not heard, not felt, and rarely touched. I was the invisible kid who could not find her own voice and I had no idea how this was going to affect my later life.

Tanks surrounded the hospital where I was born. There had been sporadic, but substantial violence in the few months leading up to my birth and I can only imagine how people were feeling at the time. Little did I know that conflict was already within me before I chose to enter this realm. What's more, they had to induce my mother's labour. A kick start to life.

Shortly after my brother arrived, and with two children in tow, my parents moved from Northern Ireland back to England. To the outside world, our life was relatively peaceful and uneventful. Education was ingrained in us at an early age; I could even say it ruled our external world. However, my inner world was in turmoil as there was virtually no space for showing or expressing emotions. I had to be seen and not heard and it wouldn't even have crossed my mind to go against the unspoken rules. I had to grin and bear it whenever I felt unfairly treated and make sure I didn't step on my father's toes. He was the breadwinner, he ruled the roost and his needs had to be tended to at all costs.

Growing up, I hated everything about myself. I hated my body, my looks, and especially my name as it was different. I wanted to be able to hide from it and have a name that didn't stick out like a sore thumb. I even hated swedes. They simply made my stomach turn. Perhaps I felt like a cross between a cabbage and a turnip myself, who knows, but my body rejected them, just like I rejected my name of Swedish origin.

Feeling different started very early, and for years it clung to me like a stick insect. At the very start of junior school, I was set apart. I was not allowed to attend the morning assembly meetings as my father didn't want me to be indoctrinated. The embarrassment I felt at having to hand in a letter to the school to excuse me from these gatherings cannot be expressed in words, not to mention the extreme humiliation of having to go all on my own to the library. I used to hide, not wanting to be seen as I dreaded having to explain to the other children why I wasn't going to assembly. I was so ashamed not to be part of the mass. To top it all, my brother was allowed to go, which I found out to my dismay when a teacher asked me why he was permitted to go and I was not. That really stung as I realised at a very young age that I was treated differently and I had no idea how to speak up.

The poignant words from my home education, 'think before you speak' were all I could hear, cutting me off from my vocal chords. Suffering in silence and holding onto my breath was the only way I knew.

It came as no surprise a few years ago when it was brought to my attention that I was the world champion at deep diving. I had been holding my breath for years. To be honest, I probably held it for most of my life as silence was my norm. Being pushed into the swimming pool at an early age by the junior school teacher, who was annoyed at my not daring to jump in and who subsequently held my head under water, obviously didn't help matters. It was just another reason for me to feel ashamed, embarrassed and inadequate.

As a teenager, I started to dream about how life could be once I had left home, yearning for that moment of freedom. When I actually left to go to university, how different I felt as I could finally rejoice in life. In fact, I took to it like a duck to water and the pressure from a strict upbringing seemed to float away. As I was relaxing, a space for joy, laughter, ease and grace had been opened and at last I started to feel alive.

The Return of Old Wounds

The plot thickened a few years later when I was reunited with my childhood emotions and the precise embodiment of that energy within me that I had blamed on my father. He was Syrian and I thought he was different, but the feelings I had already experienced as a child were to be relived for many years. It wasn't until I was an adult giving birth to our second child who had congenital heart disease, that I realised this was no coincidence, and there was a message to be received.

In 2010, my whole world changed for the better after meeting an incredible therapist. I felt joy rushing into my body, a huge 'yes' came from within as I was finally heard. I then started hearing voices and my body seemed to lift by itself to carry out the actions this inner voice was telling me to take. I was floating in a space where I had never been before as I began to listen to my own voice and deeply connect with that greater part of me.

I was in tune with my intuition. I felt permanently uplifted and I used to wake up every day full of energy and marvelling at what the universe was going to bring me that day. I was living in quantum flow. Mystical experiences became the norm, such as items disappearing, never to be found, and numerous synchronicities. But the most enigmatic incident occurred while looking at my son's homework one evening. To my astonishment, the i's were missing from all the words he had written, the o's the next day, to be followed by a different missing vowel yet again the day after. This phenomenon convinced me that a larger force was at play and the only thing I could do was to surrender. It was frightening in a way, but I was having such an exciting time observing all these signs that I had no intention of letting fear creep in.

The inner voices continued, and I was hearing "vowel … consonant … phoneme" and the sensation in my body on hearing phoneme immediately confirmed that this was what I needed to hear. The voice carried on.

"Go and look up phoneme in the dictionary, there's another meaning to it you don't know."

I immediately felt taken over by a greater force and found myself racing to the dictionary eager to find out more. I was surprised to read "an auditory hallucination in which the subject hears voices."

"OK," I thought, as I took a deep breath, "I really need to listen to you more often." It felt as if I were being spoken to from somewhere 'up there,' out in the ether. A feeling of lightness, alignment and awe came over me as if I were being divinely guided.

The excitement continued that summer when I came across Louise Hay's amazing work and devoured her book *You Can Heal Your Life*. On reading that we choose our parents and our parents choose us, something clicked into place and I realised that the pictures I was seeing on the screen of my life were my creation. Reading that physical dis-ease came from emotions stuck in the body was paradigm shifting for me. Shortly after, I was surprised to observe that I had freed myself from my eczema.

I had been riding on the crest of this wave of ascension for some time and thought that life could only get better and better; that is, until the tide turned a couple of years later…

The End of an Era

How amazing was it that my relationship of 20 years started going downhill at the same time as the war broke out in Syria? How amazing was it that the end of the world forecast for 21-12-2012 also marked the end of my former world?

In 2013, a painful change took place. My husband asked for divorce. I didn't believe what I was hearing as I was already on a path of transformation and I had convinced myself that he was part of it. I was wrong. The pain intensified and a turning point became self-evident one evening later that year.

I was in the kitchen minding my own business when a deafening noise like crashing metal nearly made me jump out of my skin. It came from the adjacent garage. A chilling sensation came over me. *What has he gone and done now?* I dreaded having to come face to face with his imposing being, but I bravely took a deep breath, braced myself and went outside.

What I found rendered me speechless. My daughter was laughing hysterically as she jumped out of her father's car, which he had just driven into mine … on purpose! Astonishment and disbelief paralysed me as I tried to make sense of what had just happened. That's when I knew the only option left was to go to the police station.

It was already late and I stewed about it before making a decision. I finally mustered up enough courage to go and do the deed

— to report him. I fought back tears, thinking how awful I was to report my own spouse, someone who had become a part of me, yet I set out on the half-hour walk there, knowing that this was it, there really was no going back. Nothing I could do, say or be was stopping his abusive behaviour and I finally had something tangible to report.

Disappointment was on the menu once again. It was late and the person in charge was not there. I had to go back the following day to put in a formal complaint. The journey back home was one of questioning, doubt and determination. I was not going to let this stop me from breaking free and after a very short night, I returned the following morning.

Once there, I just let it rip and told them the whole story, including the many years of psychological and sexual abuse, basically mentioning all his acts of violence that had left me feeling like a victim.

To my surprise, I was told that the complaint would probably not go any further as it was highly unlikely that I would be believed. I had cut myself off from feeling any emotions at that point, so thanked them for their time and felt relieved that I had actually followed through with the procedure. Little did I know at that point that I would be coming back again in only a few short months.

Breaking Open

I had gone to a gospel concert with a friend one evening in December, a rare occurrence for me as a full-time mum. I had been feeling strange that afternoon, as if something had been pushing me to go the concert. The tension had been building up in the family ever since I had reported the children's father and I was glad to have a breather.

On arriving back home, the house had an eerie feeling to it and my heart sank. *Where were the children?* I froze. Had he taken them? I desperately tried to call and message my children, but no answer. My son finally replied, telling me that they were with their father, but communication had somehow broken down. I was devastated. A long and painful court case and battle to see the children was to ensue.

As I was ploughing through this chaotic situation, something magical happened. The Divine knocked on my door at the perfect time! I was in complete awe because as my old world was leaving my space, doors opened at the same time to a magical new world of energy healing and a multitude of miraculous healing experiences.

How amazing is it that whenever a challenge shows up, I am embraced by Divine forces and an inner knowing that everything is OK?

Another wink from the universe came from my recent trip to Denmark for one of Andrea Pennington's amazing workshops. My name was recognised and had absolutely no stigma attached to it. I laughed as I was often mistaken for a local and nobody had any difficulty in pronouncing my name. I sensed that that part of me had shifted and it was yet another example indicating that my outer world is forever reflecting back to me whatever I am feeling on the inside. I had invited a different scenario into my life by fully accepting that part of me.

These past few years have shown me that the greatest gift I can give to others is taking care of myself, finding my path of joy and what lights me up in order to enable others to do the same. If I hold back from myself, then I hold back from my children too.

I recognise that I am yet to fully embrace my soul in my experience, but I feel so peaceful knowing that everything is happening *for* me and not *to* me so that I can become the greatest version of myself. I find it so fascinating that the universe is always responding to the vibrational frequency I am emitting and that when the underlying energy of any challenging situation is transmuted, the stories from the past collapse as there is nothing holding them in place anymore.

I am truly grateful for every actor who has played, is playing and will play a role on stage in the projection of my life, from the seemingly big bad wolves to the fairy godmothers. And funnily enough, there are no more big bad wolves, only beautiful co-creators, as are you, reading this story.

You have infinite potential and the power to transform your world.

About the Author

Karin is a Lightworker, mystic, energy healer, and empath. After profoundly transformational experiences in 2010, she caught glimpses of her Higher Self and saw that it is possible to put a stop to all pain and suffering in the world. She opened up to infinite human potential, realised that magic is all around us and committed to becoming a true vibrational catalyst in order to help raise the vibration of the planet and empower others on their ascension path.

Karin now helps people to deeply connect with their Higher Self in order to create a life of unconditional love, flow, and inner peace.

To connect with Karin:
Email: karin.eke@free.fr
Tel: +33783520047
theascensionpath.com

You can also find Karin on Facebook and Instagram:
facebook.com/karinm.eke
facebook.com/groups/985205621653689
instagram.com/karin_eke

Discovering My Erotic Self

Gila Nehemia

"What you seek is seeking you" ~ Rumi

It was two o'clock in the afternoon on a cool October day in 2013. My husband and I returned home from the hospital after receiving the dismal news that the cancerous tumor in his stomach was growing. He had been in remission for four months.

We accepted the news without words; our eyes met with disappointment. He bought me a Swarovski necklace in the hospital lobby as we left. The clear and precious pearls lay softly against my neck. It was his way of showing his love for me.

At home, we wanted nothing more than to push the news aside and bask in sweet love making; the only thing that truly mattered. Wearing only the necklace, I unabashedly walked around looking in the mirror, fully aware that the porch curtains were still open. I admired my lithe body showcasing the precious pearls. I knew the kids would come home in a few hours so I could not remain in this revelry much longer.

When reality set in again, I found myself feeling distraught. The recurrence was not a complete surprise, though it was still unwelcome news.

My husband had decided not to undergo further chemotherapy treatment and I understood. I could not blame him for wanting to avoid the pain caused by all those toxic medications; not a second time.

So together we vowed to accept whatever hand fate dealt us. It was the end of this degrading struggle and the beginning of my journey into the NOW!

His cancer was a poison that manifested itself in all the emotional trappings of a man in dire pain. For me, it was simply a trap. I felt sucked into a life I did not deserve and could not escape.

Seeing him like this did not discount the 17 years of abuse I'd endured as his personal punching bag. He had a temper that he not only raged against me but also against our children.

When the kids got home the tension in the air was thick and unabating. They went to their room while my husband and I sat on the bed in silence.

Despite everything could I accept his departure from this world? One minute I loved him, the next we were arguing. And then the violence. How did I allow this to happen for all these years? Who was I kidding? How can love include fear?

My body was throbbing. My fear choked my voice. I felt powerless, as if I were being gagged. An hour later, he apologized. Just like all the other times.

My emotions were chaotic, up and down on the chart. How do I keep myself and my children safe? I can't leave him now, he is dying. I left to go shopping, crying in the car. What should I do? Every night I get up. He can't sleep, his body hurts, I call doctors to help with the pain. We write down each medication, what time, and what he took.

I am taking the leap of faith. I am not fighting anymore. I am assisting my husband on his journey. I cry a lot.

Why is it that everyone leaves me? My mom, my dad, my husband? They all died before my eyes. What did I do wrong? What is the message I must learn?

In each of these relationships I felt trapped. My desire to be me was never fulfilled, it was like a fire being quenched each time with water. The ember burned low, brightly at times but the coals remained hot. I knew when I married him 16 years ago that it wasn't quite right, but said yes anyway. I was honoring my commitment, yet I was dead and barely breathing. This was not the life I wanted to live.

The next few months were a whirlwind. My husband died in May of 2014. My kids and I buried him in his hometown in Israel and we immigrated there to live near his family. After two years of grieving, I began to pick myself up. I dated a few men but the relationships were disastrous. I kept feeling like I wanted to fill a void and each time I was disappointed; a repeated pattern in my life. Each time, I numbed myself with each man that I dated.

I decided to change the pattern for myself and my children. I needed to love myself. Nobody can love me, all of me, if I do not love myself in totality.

Who am I? A philosophical question I pondered my whole life, throughout my world travels, and my study of philosophy and literature. I fed my quest for truth by studying different cultures, religions, and spiritual texts when I was young, yet at 48 I was still searching. After attending a life changing course of releasing old fears and a self-imposed belief in victimization, I sent out an intention to the Universe to send me my true love.

I supported this intention with affirmations and consistently doing what I loved, cherishing my body and my love of freedom and adventure. I spent time with my beloved children embracing my spontaneity and love of nature. I spent time alone with my dog, taking long nature walks. A couple of months later, I decided to go out in the dating world and give it another try.

I swiped right on my phone in the dating app in April 2016. Hot days were already here in Israel. I was looking for a younger man, despite my small questioning voice that said I am a responsible mother of three. My intuition guided me to look for someone I met a year ago online. Will I find him?

A few days later he contacted me. I texted back. It was an easy banter. He got sexual within a couple of days, I declined his advances. He apologized and changed his tune. Intrigued, I continued to converse. Butterflies were flitting and floating in my stomach, messages from my gut. I listened. I didn't even know him, yet he felt familiar. My body trusted and my mind questioned. I gave into a passionate sexual energy, unquenched by previous partners.

We were talking for a few days. I asked him to call me, told him I needed to hear his voice. He called, we spoke for 3 hours about everything and anything. I felt like I was speaking to myself, I felt really comfortable for the first time in my life. He knew how to entice me, say the right words to get me desiring more, it felt "real" for the first time.

What was this feeling? It was more than just desire, it felt familiar, soulful. I couldn't wait to meet him in person. My body was feeling light, my sexual center was flooded with endorphins. I sent him a voice message after I woke up. I felt like I had made love to his energy and yet I hadn't yet touched his body. There was an inexplicable connection.

The next day I drove to his home. He was waiting for me. He got in on the passenger side and we parked the car together in unpretentious silence. I felt safe in his presence. We walked side by side to his house. Just being next to him I could feel the sexual tension building.

We made a fruit shake together, cutting fruit, cleaning up, and getting high from the healing properties of the trees imbibed in our drinks.

As we sat beside each other, I was wet, the tigress within me opened up portals that were previously closed. My mind raced.

'Hold on, you don't want to make a mistake...'

My desires dismissed the security warnings and gave in to the passion. I relished in the thought of sharing divine experiences with this person, his unique energy; it was about to change my life forever.

My primal nature – untamed, wild, and raw – came flooding to the surface. I could not stop myself. I pushed logic aside and gave in to the inner creative vortex. I let go of my fear and I surrendered to the sheer passion of the moment, which lasted hours, yet it felt mere seconds. Position, after position, taking breaths only to allow more oxygen to fuel the desire and passion that enveloped our sacred time together.

It was not only the unbridled passion that kept me desiring more, it was the conflict that tied me to the connection. We respectfully discussed our issues. We allowed each other to be vulnerable about our pain. The connection guided me to truly heal my old "victim" patterns. I no longer saw him in human form, but as an energetic force that gelled with mine. In his presence I was able to be at my worst and my best and every color in between. It was love without conditions or expectations. An organic soulful love that left me reeling after each meeting.

I thought I had loved before
Though, I never felt so joyful and burgeoning with possibilities
I realized that only when I truly loved and accepted myself

My heart expanded like the earth soaking in the nourishment after a torrential rain

My heart opened up like a flower and remembered

A love so pure like the water flowing from a hot spring

A love so deep as the darkness near the ocean floor

For as we shed cloaks that were holding us back

We danced magically, seeing only each other

Our hearts were finally free

From our minds to feel the love that was reserved for each other

Our synergetic connection uncovered layers of pain that had been trapped in my body. The unfolding fear of men, oppression, hiding, judgement, denial, and entrapment began to be healed. What started as an interlude went on for over a year and a half.

Fleeting texts, meetings in nature, music, poems, freedom to love, freedom to be authentically me. My creative juices were flowing in ways I never witnessed before. I let go of what didn't serve me. Leaving my day job and starting a new business based on the divine power of my desires. My feminine sexual life force was using my creative, authentic self as a source of my power. I was transforming before my eyes into the person I was meant to be.

I listened to my intuition, the divine wisdom of my body. I received divine downloads from the clouds, nature, birds, my soul animals and friends. My relationships changed. My children became more emotional, loving, felt more safe around me and our relatives. Other people left my life, or their advice did not sway me. I trusted in me, my inner voice, my divinity. I manifested my desires more quickly. I believed in my dreams, I became limitless.

A year later, in March 2018, as my business grew, I had a setback; spiraling downwards. My financial situation was out of control. I sat in my room, crying on the floor at my growing debt. How can I keep paying the rent? How will I take care of my children? Do I have to go back to work in a corporate job? What am I going to do? I cried relentlessly, praying to God. Seeing only my lack of money, not realizing that other choices exist.

I had already asked my family members for help so I did not want to ask for more. I did not see a way out. In addition, my soulful lover and I got into a fight. Distraught and confused I began to delve into the depths of myself. Loving myself erotically was the only answer, the one thing I did not fully explore. I realized the divinity is within myself. In order to truly live my manifestations I had to let go of my attachments, to surrender them to the Divine, to lose all control.

I received a call from a coach in June 2018. She promised me that all my dreams would come true, because she saw it intuitively. She validated my feelings, my belief that everything will be okay; she supported me. She struck a chord in me. She felt familiar, like I already knew her. How was I going to pay her? What could I do to make this happen? I realized once I commit to the Universe the Universe supports my dream tenfold.

Her words were divine, they spoke to the little scared girl inside me that thought I was worthless, weak and penniless. I mustered up the courage to face my inner child and soothe her. I told her that we will emerge victorious, stronger than ever before. I began to liquidate my pension funds and made decisions to go to a women's retreat in Spain.

Miraculously money began to flow my way, more than I imagined. I paid my coach. I went to the retreat that changed my life. I met like-minded women that shared my belief that our bodies were meant to be erotic vessels to serve the divine. We all believed that we are meant to experience human pleasure to connect to our own divinity. I openly sat naked and experienced orgasmic bliss all alone, among other women without having sex.

I made love to myself through my breath, sacred erotic practices, a trust in my purpose, and sacred acts of loving my body in nature. I confidently spoke of my mission, my writing, my experiences with other women in the retreat. As the days went by I felt lighter, more centered, more magnetic and more in love with myself, my body, and my consciousness. I left the retreat committed to my purpose, my dreams, my ideal mate and my soul family.

I also had a unique healing experience at the retreat by the grace of a gifted healer. She channeled a message from my late husband to me. I realized he was indeed an angel, for his presence brought me to speak my truth, the mission of living a life in the paradigm of LOVE. He wanted me to stand up for myself, so he could finally escape the mental trappings of his own existence. I was too afraid at the time, yet I felt so loved realizing the truth. It was exhilarating; a knowing that my whole life was part of a spiritual mission, to assist the collective to live and love freely. All he ever wanted, all I ever wanted was to be ME.

Even my kids noticed a change. They mentioned how I came home a new woman. I spontaneously went to the beach with them at night. Freely and lovingly they played in the warm Mediterranean Sea with very few souls venturing into the waves. The beach was empty and they stayed close to the shore. My loyal dog guarded us as we shrieked joyfully in the warm winds, the night sky empty of people and full of healing energy. The waves represented my surrender to the Divine; my unconditional trust that I will be held and cherished amidst the chaos. A message that my dreams and desires are the map of my soul. I listened, followed and trusted my inner guidance.

The clouds beckoned me to arise
Showing me divine messages in the sky
"Come with me" they gesticulate
I listen and I look at the dense vehicle opening
Beyond the shape
Beyond the billowing softness
Beyond the blue turquoise expansiveness
I see a world calling my soul
Heed the signal
Step into the portal
Bathe in the knowing
Of the divine unfolding of each moment
Of the anticipation and the excitement
As my path slowly emerges
Through the releasing of layers and layers of love hidden in my heart

If this story resonated with you, I invite you to schedule a free 30 minute Strategy call with me. It is your choice to change the old patterns in your life that keep you repeating the same story. Change your story, love yourself erotically and watch as your life transforms.

About the Author

Gila Nehemia is a spiritual erotic poet, writer, coach, and wise woman. She's passionate about empowering people to experience a Sacred Erotic Love partnership within and without. She believes that conscious erotic self-love changes the paradigm of love relationships in a person's inner and outer circles.

As a Shamanic healer, Gila loves nature and uses its inherent healing properties to heal herself and her loved ones. She holds Sacred Circles for women to provide support and divine transmission. She believes we're all on this earth to help each other grow and to radiate our light and love onto the world.

Find out more about Gila's services visit:
www.wildwritersheal.com

To schedule a free call visit:
bookeroticsession.as.me/schedule.php?appointmentType=7182730

3
How Trauma & Illness Open the Door to New Life

Sometimes the illnesses we face do not have an organic cause. The body is an instrument which can speak to us in many ways. Sometimes the language the body communicates with involves pain, illness or a general sense of *dis-ease*.

Because the body and mind are really one comprehensive unit, the troubled emotional states, anxiety, overwhelm and depression can be seen as communication tools used to alert us to the need for change. The body reminds us of our immortality and can open the door to transformation on many levels. And many of find that bearing witness to the end of someone's life in the body can inspire us to live more fully, and even remove fear of death.

The body-mind can be magical instruments of intuition as well. And when we learn to heed the messages the body sends we can recover and heal faster, bounce back after challenges and evolve on our spiritual path.

Trauma exists in the tissues of our body, including the brain. When traditional medicine doesn't quite fix us, and when conventional diagnostic tools fail to reveal some physical cause for our discomfort, we can look to our past experiences, our internal values and beliefs for clues.

The Journey from Fear to Freedom

Abbie Persall

*"When the world pushes you to your knees,
you're in the perfect position to pray"* ~ Rumi

If I were told 10 years ago about the challenges I would face as I turned 50, I would never have believed I would have the strength and resilience to not only survive, but transform my pain and loss into hope and love. My journey unfolds.

The Tumor

In January 2012, a few weeks before my 50th birthday, I was feeling very tired. I made a visit to my gynecologist and shared with her my lack of energy and feelings of depression. I blamed my fatigue on the fact that my 35-year marriage was ending in divorce.

A few blood tests later, I received a call from my doctor to discuss the results. It appeared I had low thyroid. My doctor suggested I see an endocrinologist in Los Angeles. I was diagnosed with Hashimoto's disease. He suggested an MRI of my pituitary gland to rule out a tumor.

Two weeks later I had the scan and the next day shared my 50th birthday in the mountains with my family. The following week I went back to the doctor to review the results. She said, "Good news, you don't have a tumor on your pituitary. However you do have what we call a meningioma, a benign brain tumor."

119

I was floored.

The doctor said we could just watch it since in most cases it doesn't have to be removed. She suggested I see a neurologist to get a second opinion. I felt numb as I left her office. I thought, "this cannot be happening to me."

I made the appointment to see the neurologist, who then referred me to see a neurosurgeon. Fear was quickly becoming my constant companion.

As days turned into weeks and weeks into months, I did my best to rise above the fear and uncertainty. After three months, I had a second MRI. By this time the tumor was stable.

I had an MRI every three to six months for over two years. Fear was running my life. I was consumed by the thought of something foreign living inside my head. I had lost myself in this darkness of fear.

MY Best Friend, My Mother

In June 2012, I moved from my beautiful home on a golf course and completely ended my 35-year marriage. I remember lying on the floor in my closet crying out to God, "Why now? Why a tumor?"

I finally let go of a marriage that hadn't worked for many years. I had been living in a self-imposed prison of fear and only I held the key to my freedom. I was finally willing to unlock the door, in hopes of a new life, a new self. I had the strength to end it and now this. The pain in my heart was unbearable.

I moved into a new home with my beautiful mother. Mom had some health issues and I felt it best for her to be closer to me. She was an incredible spirit, so alive, intelligent, witty. She moved in with me in June, and three months later she suffered a massive stroke. She was left unable to speak. A tragic outcome for a woman who loved and valued intelligent and meaningful conversations.

She was able to understand most of what was said to her but her comprehension was greater when paired with the spoken and written word. She would communicate by writing, though her writing was fragmented. I became her interpreter. My protector and my rock now needed me to provide the same security she had given to me over the years.

I remember many nights when I came home from work, I would sit with mom on the couch while she played solitaire on her laptop. She looked so sad; her beautiful face showing a life lived, sorrows felt, joys embraced, with each laugh line, each crease within the silhouette of her face. I could see that life, as it does to all of us, had taken a toll on her body.

Life leaves its markings on us, time ticks so slowly for the young and so rapidly for the elderly. I knew what this was doing to her, the pain of realizing her life now was forever altered. Never, never, would she have thought her story would end this way.

The cloak of loneliness was very real and very palpable on those evenings sitting together. It seemed we were the only ones in the universe. No one could see the interaction or feel the pain as I watched this strong woman reverting to an almost childlike state.

You see, mom was extraordinary. She was my best friend, the most attentive listener and giver of wisdom, and now she was silenced. Yet, true to her being, she would still show that spark, and would rally to the call of joy. She would clap her hands, smile and take my arm when she wanted to show me something, and write down all her thoughts as best as she could.

The Call

November 2013, at 1:30 in the morning, I received a call from the police department. They asked if I had a brother, named Pete. I said yes, as my heart dropped into my stomach. I knew what was coming. The police said my brother and only sibling was found dead in his car on the side of the road. My brother had been fighting the demon of heroin addiction for many years. He was only 52.

I now had the responsibility to tell my mother that her beautiful son was now gone. As she walked into the kitchen that morning, I asked her to sit down, I said I had something I needed to share with her. She was happy, so unaware of what I was about to say.

I told her what happened and then wrote the same words on a sheet of paper. She sat there shaking her head, as I placed my arms around her and said, "I am so sorry, Mom."

We cried, knowing for years this was coming. Maybe the stroke in some way, was a blessing, maybe it lessened the pain bearing down on her. I don't know. I do know she loved him and missed him and struggled for many years trying to help him.

After a while, I could see the sadness deepening within her. You see, she wanted to live back on the golf course where she and my father had lived. Something told me, "Take her home, Abbie. Take her back where her soul feels at peace."

I surrendered. I listened to her, and together we made it happen. I look back now, and I think she guided me. It was her strength that helped me to help her get where she needed to be.

I worked out the details and within a few days, she moved back into her same neighborhood. She became text savvy and

would answer her phone, with a joyful sound. We had a system --
a hum for yes and a win-win, the sound she made for no.

Surgery

In March 2014, I had finally decided I could not live in fear
and uncertainty any longer. I began having sensory seizures, and
to my dismay, I was placed on seizure medication. After, review-
ing several doctors and hospitals I decided to have my surgery at
UC San Francisco.

I scheduled the tumor removal for May 21, 2014. It all
seemed so unreal to me. Me, Abbie, getting my skull cut open.
The uncertainty of what they would find, not knowing if I would
be able to walk or raise my hand. Not knowing how my life could
or would be altered. I believe I was in a state of awe, somewhat
numb, yet something, some inner force, strength, kept me mov-
ing forward. As I know now, it was my spirit and the spirit that
governs this universe, a power greater than myself, which I could
not explain.

A month prior I knew I needed something to help me walk
through this tunnel of complete uncertainty and lack of control. I
could run to every professional and ask them to reassure me that
I would be okay. Yet, the truth was, not one human being on this
planet could give me any guarantee because, you see, they were
not ultimately in charge. I believe the universe works through
people, but in the end they are still human and very, very fallible.

One day I found myself sitting on a yoga mat, listening to
beautiful music and watching the others around me breathing and
chanting, moving in a way I had never seen in a yoga class before.
The funny thing is that it felt right, it felt like home. I cried on
that mat. I cried for my life, for my mother, for my brother, for
my children, I cried for me. It was on that day that I knew no

matter what happened, I would be okay, I would make it through this challenge with a soul full of the wonder for this life I was given. It was with this belief I entered into surgery.

I woke up, with a tube coming out of the top of my head. I could raise my leg and my arm. I felt so blessed and thankful. But within 24 hours, something changed. I wasn't able to pick up a cup. I called the doctor and immediately they sent me down for a CAT scan.

I felt like Frankenstein, blood in my hair, stitches from the top of my head down the side of my skull. Oddly, I felt exposed, but also so open to the experience. As I was being wheeled down the hall, another man was being wheeled in the opposite direction. He had brain surgery too. We locked eyes and smiled at each other. It was as though we knew each other deeply without ever saying a word. After surgery, the doctors discovered a blood clot, but in time and with physical therapy, I would recover my motor skills.

Death

September 11, 2014, four months after my surgery, my beautiful mother passed away. As the universe would have it, she died on my brother's birthday. Two days before she died, as she laid in her hospital bed, she reached up and patted my head, speaking in her utterances and smiling. I knew what she was saying, I knew she was telling me that I was going to be okay.

On the morning of her death I had entered the hospital, stopping first to use the restroom 100 feet from the ICU were she was resting. While in the restroom, I heard over the loudspeaker, "Code blue in bed 8." In my mind I frantically counted the beds and realized she was in bed 8. I rushed to the phone outside of the ICU, called the nurse and said, "This is Abbie Persall. Is my mom okay? I heard you call a code blue. Can I see her?"

She told me to please go down the hall and wait in the waiting room until someone came to talk to me. A woman came toward me and said she was the social worker and that they were doing all they could for my mom. I knew then her life was ending. Within a few minutes, the social worker came back and said, "I am sorry, your mother has passed."

I sobbed. The loss I felt was indescribable. I asked to see her. As I entered the room, my eyes gazed upon her body. The life, the spirit, the voice that made my mother, my mother, was gone. Yet, where did she go? Who was this person I was looking at? Where was her smile, her jokes, her strength? Did they simply vanish when she sipped her last breath? No, I thought.

We are more than our bodies; these are merely suits we carry as we walk through life. My mother was more than her body. Her body was the vessel through which her spirit would shine. The essence of who my mother was lived deep within her soul, deep beyond this human flesh. As I gazed around the room, I reached down to touch her hair and kiss her forehead, and as I did I whispered to her, "I know you are not of this body, I know Mom."

The moment the words left my lips, I felt a rush, like a fast brush of wind which caught my attention. I felt her spirit leave the crown of her head and fly through the wall. I was shocked. I am a very open spiritual person, but I have never witnessed or felt any spiritual experience or phenomenon like that before.

I knew then, for certain, there is a power, a force, a soulful existence beyond this earthly body. I knew, not because I read it or hoped for it, I knew because I had just experienced it. Mom's soul had waited for me to arrive at the hospital. Her soul waited for me to kiss her and tell her I knew she now was not of this earthly realm and she was free to transition on to her next journey.

Resilience Through Faith

As one journey ends a new one begins. Here now, in 2018, four years post brain surgery, four years walking this earth without my most loving compassionate friend, my mother, I have found myself more grounded, more confident, more awake with faith and hope that life will sustain us all.

We can meet this human condition while embracing the strength within our souls. I am proud of the journey I have walked thus far. I know Mom is proud of my journey as well.

If I can give anything to anyone through these words I share, may you know and hear the beauty in this song called Life. Its melody may at times veer off key, but know that with love, patience and small doses of hope and faith the melody will find its harmony once again.

Let your soul sing your song. May you be courageous and soar. Seize this life and every drop of nectar within it. May your journey begin anew, with each breath of life.

About the Author

Abbie Persall is a passionate educator, working to bring change to the educational system by using mindfulness and soulful connection when working with students and adults. She is a school counselor, a Kundalini Yoga Instructor, and holds a Master's Degree in Special Education. It is Abbie's passion to support others in accessing the guru within.

The answers we seek have been with us all along. Holding space for others to feel safe in being who they truly were met to be, is a gift not only for one's self, but for others who journey across your path.

Please reach out with any questions or comments to:
abbie.persall@yahoo.com

The Wisdom of Our Body, Mind & Spirit

Joyce Wazirali

How I Healed From Glaucoma

I t was 2013. I was a single mom with two kids and running my own business. For more than one week, my inner voice told me to go to an optician to measure the pressure of my eye. For some reason I believed it to be extremely high and felt I needed to do something about it.

Of course, the practical me thought, "It's my imagination." But the warnings of my inner voice didn't let up. You see, I have a strong intuition that gives me answers and warns me if there is something wrong with my health. It even signals whether disaster is afoot affecting my life, the lives of my loved ones and even my clients. So I went to my optician to stop the internal nagging. After all, I had no pain in my eyes and my vision was good. I had nothing to worry about.

My optician measured my eye pressure. He told me that he normally measured eye pressure starting at the age of fifty years. I was younger. That's why he'd never measured my eye pressure before. At first he couldn't measure the pressure and he thought that perhaps something was wrong with the device. So to test it, he measured his own and his colleague's eye pressure. Both were normal. My optician got worried. He told me that my eye pressure would be either extremely high or low. I wasn't worried because I didn't feel any pain and I could see normally.

To measure my eye pressure, he had to call the manufacturer of the device. After receiving a few instructions he was able to take the measurements, but this only gave him cause for concern. My pressure was twice that of a normal eye. The highest value is normally 20 and mine was 37 in both eyes. He strongly suggested I see an eye specialist and gave me a recommendation.

That day I came home and I still couldn't believe what happened. My inner voice was right again. I started to cry. At the one hand I felt gratitude for the warning of my inner voice and on the other hand uncertainty about the outcome.

A few days later, I had an appointment with my eye specialist. Let's call him Joe. The walls of Joe's waiting room were decorated with diplomas. I had never seen so many. I thought, "He must be very good." On the tables were folders with information about eye diseases. Sitting in the waiting room for my turn I saw only elderly patients; most were about seventy years and older. I was only forty eight. Again I thought, "This must be a mistake."

When it was my turn Joe examined my eyes and told me that the eye measurement of the optician was right. They'd caught it just in time. Any later and my optic nerves would have been destroyed because of the high pressure in my eye ball. When damaged, the optic nerves never recover and in the end you can actually go blind! He said most people discover it too late because they don't feel it.

He explained that most patients come to the eye specialist when they have lost eyesight or have the feeling that they are looking through a tube. Some become blind. The eye specialist gave compliments to my optician. I told him that I went to the optician to do an eye ball pressure measurement because of my inner voice. Then he said, "You've got a good intuition. Keep listening to it."

Joe then told me that I had glaucoma and would have to use eyedrops for the rest of my life to keep my eye ball pressure normal. He told me I had the least dangerous form of the condition. He also gave me a folder with information about glaucoma. Joe said, "From now on, you're a glaucoma patient."

I felt shocked. I thought, "How is this possible? I meditate, practice Nichiren Buddhism and Kriya Yoga every day. I don't drink alcohol, don't smoke cigarettes, I take good care of myself, do my workouts and always work on my self development. How is this possible?"

I was told that I had no choice but to use prescription eyedrops. The side effects were extreme. After I started to use the drops, my eyes became light-sensitive and I developed dark spots under them. I felt tired but my eye lashes were growing (actually, this was the only positive side effect). I had problems with my teeth and had to visit the dentist regularly. I even had pain in my bones along with several other complaints.

Not long after I started using the eye drops, I went to a seminar. My concentration was very poor and I hoped that no one would ask me questions. During a presentation the light of the laser pointer was very intense, I couldn't keep my eyes open. I just looked down on my papers and held my hands before my eyes to keep the intense light from irritating me. At the other hand, I couldn't very well close them or I would fall asleep in the middle of the seminar. I didn't understand what was happening to me. I got very worried about my situation.

One morning I was due to conduct a workshop with twelve participants but I didn't feel well so I called the general practice centre. The doctor there told me that I had symptoms of heart failure. *What?*

He urged me to immediately stop using the eye drops saying that if I continued I'd be doing so at my own risk. Since the heart failure symptoms began after I started the eyedrops, I made a big decision. Knowing that my eye ball pressure would rise again I had to decide if continuing to use them was worth the risk.

That day was very difficult for me. I gave the workshop, not knowing if I would have a heart attack in the middle of my lecture. The only comforting thought was that at least I had twelve people who could help me if something did happen.

Then I had this realisation:

> If I keep using these eye drops, I would become handicapped, thus needing a wheelchair. I would have no income, and I'd have to move to a house without stairs.

> If I stop using the eye drops, I would become blind. I wasn't fifty years old yet and as a single mom, I had nobody to take care of me and my two kids needed me. I have to take care of my kids and see them grow up. If I become blind, my world would become very small. I couldn't paint anymore or enjoy the beautiful coulors of the nature. No more holidays…

I began thinking about how precious my eyes are to me. They are my window to the world. The idea of losing my eyesight made me insecure and I didn't share my situation or my fears with anyone. However, once I stopped using the eyedrops, the side effects disappeared.

The next day I went to Joe the optician to check my eye ball pressure. It was normal. I told him about the side effects and the fact that I stopped using the eye drops. His advice was to keep using them and to cope with the side effects. The other option was to have an eye operation. But he advised against it. It was too dangerous, he said. The only thing he could do was to give me a prescription for different eyedrops. These turned out to be heavier than the first ones.

That day I actually felt a difference in my eyes; the difference between high eye pressure and normal eye pressure. (You can compare the difference I felt with a frog in a pan with cold water. When the water gets slowly heated, the frog will not feel any danger and it will die. But when you throw a frog in hot water, it will feel the danger and immediately jump out.)

Since I could now detect the difference between high and normal eye ball pressure, which, by the way, is not normally possible, I was sure I could rely on my feelings. I went to the drugstore with my prescription and took the new eyedrops home. First, I read all the side effects. I was shocked.

My inner voice told me, *"If I use these stronger eye drops it would cause a lot of suffering and maybe even my death. A painful death."*

I was confused, not knowing what to do. I thought, "There should be another solution; a natural way. My eyes were trying to tell me something." So I started to communicate with my inner voice which warned me about this. And as usual, I followed its lead.

My optician advised me to read a book about eye problems and to do exercises to cure my eye problems. I read the book and did different exercises every day, but it didn't help.

So I went to my general practitioner who has a scientific background with an anthroposophical vision about health care. Anthroposophy is a formal educational and therapeutic system established by Rudolf Steiner, which seeks to use mainly natural means to optimize physical and mental health and well-being.

I told him the whole story. That's when I realized that he was the first person I'd told the story of what was happening with my health and the warnings I had been having. He turned out to be exactly the right person because he brought me closer to a solution. He knew an eye specialist who worked with eye drops that had no side effects. I'll just call him 'Harry', my second eye specialist.

I went to Harry for research. He was a scientific eye specialist with a holistic view about health care. He gave me a prescription for his eye drops to use instead of the ones that had caused me so much discomfort. I wouldn't mind using these for the rest of my life as long as I did not have side effects.

After a half year I went to Harry to check my eye ball pressure. The pressure was normal and I had no side effects. I was so thankful and gave him a big hug. There was hope. I could continue to use my windows to the world, to take care of my kids and see them grow and bloom like beautiful flowers. I could continue with my practice, I wouldn't have to move, and I could even go on holiday. I felt relieved and my heart overflowed with love and joy.

But all that changed when I went to Harry for my second checkup. He said he had good and bad news for me. The good news was that the pressure was still normal. The bad news was that his colleagues had forbidden him to prescribe the eye drops anymore because they had not been scientifically tested. So there was my next challenge. I had to find a way to cure my eyes in a natural way. I had to get rid of the glaucoma without medicine.

As a therapist, I have helped many clients heal from health problems who were once told they had to live with their diagnosis. Now I had to use that wisdom on myself. With my scientific and holistic education I started to merge these two worlds together and I have had many experiences of miraculous healings using the wisdom of those two worlds.

From the scientific point of view, I began to delve into the causes of glaucoma. There is a circular muscle in the eyeball which regulates the pressure. When this muscle does not function properly the eyeball pressure will get too high or too low.

From the holistic point of view, when we experience a trauma, the muscles in our body become strained. When it's in the shoulder a massage can sometimes remove the tension. When the tension is in a place in your body where you can't massage it will stay there. So I thought, "I can't massage the circular muscle in my eye ball. So I have to find another way to remove the tension."

I believe in the wisdom of our body, mind and spirit. I also believe that our body stores our experiences. They say that 'our eyes are the mirror of our soul.' So I thought, a trauma on the soul level could cause tension in the eyes.

I set out to do some body work and trauma healing. I went to an osteopath who activated my self-healing ability. I asked colleagues to guide me through my self-made program of visualization and imagination to discover the trauma stored in my body, to heal it and to get some insight to take with me as a pearl in the here and now.

With my own tailor-made program of trauma healing on the physical, emotional, rational, spiritual and soul level, I solved the cause of my eyeball pressure. For years now my eye pressure has remained normal. I don't use medicines and my optic nerves are intact. I am officially cured from glaucoma.

Lessons learned:

1. If you have a strong inner voice, keep listening to it.
2. Never give up.
3. Stay curious; it contains the word cure.
4. Use the wisdom of your Body, Mind, Spirit and the Physician.

5. If massage doesn't help, find a good therapist.

6. When the scientific and holistic worlds merge, miracles can happen.

7. Stay in tune with what you're feeling in your body.

About the Author

Joyce Wazirali is an author and a holistic therapist for both individuals and businesses. Her company, Heliotropo, focuses on solving traumas that often prevent patients from realizing their full potential. She helps them gain strength and equips them with the power to move forward.

Heliotropo came to be after 30 years of study and experience with people, business development and growth, through coaching, counselling, teambuilding activities, cultural change and co-creation.

Once she was one of two co-founders and director of a company in business services which flourished in 13 years to a company with 80 staff members.

With her multicultural, medical, scientific, financial and holistic background, she can tailor a program that combines insight and integration with diagnostics and healing.

Joyce's vision is: 'man is a unique and versatile creature, with deep answers for a happy life.'

For more information:
Email: info@heliotropo.nl
www.heliotropo.nl

From Pain to Painting

Stine Moe Engelsrud

That Pain Thing!

It was early in the morning, and I woke up with pain. The pain was dark, bitter, noisy and unwelcome, and it had been with me for too long now. It entered my life in 2009, when I was pregnant with my fourth child, and it had shown no signs of leaving. Over the years, it felt like the pain was an alien taking over my life.

I was really looking forward to getting some relief from the pain after my upcoming hip replacement surgery. I was hoping they would fix me. But, even after the surgery, my body was in such bad condition, there was no real hope for a quick recovery.

As a result, I continued having pain as my companion. The pain made me feel constantly unhappy and uneasy, and it made it impossible for me to make any plans for the day — or for my life in general. It felt like pain was eating me up on the inside. I felt my body was hijacked by pain, and it drained me of all energy.

Even though I had this very uneasy and unpleasant feeling about pain, I felt it was my companion, but I had no way of making peace with it. It was a constant struggle, like a war going on between us, one I couldn't win. Exhausted from carrying this partner around all day, it forced me to bed early.

Pain was getting the best of me. Years with this powerful and unfriendly companion seriously pushed me towards the edge of wanting to give up on life. If it hadn't been for my beautiful kids and husband, I think I would have gone spiraling down towards the end. But the thought of leaving my kids, and forcing them to live with an open wound in their life, was not an option. Just having such a thought jumping around in my mind shows how desperate I was. I really struggled to find anything meaningful to do with my life, and that didn't make it easier to choose to carry on.

Over the years, I used every trick I knew to get back on my feet. Putting on a brave face and pulling myself together was my go-to technique. But after a while it was no longer a viable option. I'd let my body endure all sorts of painful and heavy treatments over too many years. The hip replacement was only the last in a series of injuries that had weighed me down.

I was afraid I couldn't endure any more pain and suffering. It felt like I somehow needed to make a shift in my approach. I needed something that would maybe make me feel good again, and the one thing that crossed my mind was a good old massage. I remember when I did gymnastics in my younger years we gave each other massages after the training, and that brought back some good memories.

I found the number to a health clinic near my home, and was looking forward to finding a moment where pain and I could make peace. Interestingly, looking at it in retrospect, I see that this was a major shift in my ideology. Shifting from pushing my body to cope with life through pain to giving it a gentle massage instead.

The skilled massage therapist that met me on that surprisingly sunny Tuesday in spring three years ago, was Hanne Elviken. I remember that I liked her instantly, even though I felt a bit intimidated by her. She looked so strong, muscular and beautiful with her long curly hair and her warm soul filling the room.

I collapsed onto her massage table, not really interested in sharing my story with her. But while I was lying there on the table taking in every single detail of where her hands touched, the smell in the room and how hot it felt in there, I finally loosened up and felt more relaxed.

She asked me a few questions about my life, and that got me to thinking. It didn't take long before she touched me in a way that made me feel like my whole defense mechanism collapsed, and tears started running down my face. A little shy and uncomfortable about crying so openly, I was still trying to hide it the best way I could. I had learned that showing tears was something you just don't do.

Hanne told me there were no medals of honor given for fighting so hard against my own body. She promised to stand by my side and get me back on my feet by the end of the summer, that is, if I wanted her help. She said, "I am going to give you the treatments for free, because I really want to help you. But then you have to listen to my advice and follow it."

My initial thought was that it was too good to be true. I had endured too many bad experiences when accepting offers from others. It usually ended up costing me more than I really wanted to pay. But somehow, deep down, I felt like I could trust her, and I felt comfortable laying my life in her hands.

Three months zoomed by in the fast lane, and by the end of the summer I had learned some important lessons. The most important thing was listening to my inner voice. I learned to do this by tapping into what I liked. Hanne told me to do more things I enjoyed. The first time she told me this, I was a bit puzzled, because I didn't know how to define what I liked or disliked. But the first time I felt that enjoyment in my body, I quickly realized that I had been spending my life doing what I thought was expected of me, and not living the life that I had inside of me, the life my soul craved. Last but not least, Hanne gave the phrase unconditional love real meaning for me.

A new morning was emerging and I felt like a different person. I had grown a pair of special ears to listen to what my body was telling me, and I turned to different people for help to get more finely tuned guidance in how to fully embrace and align with my soul's purpose. In retrospect, I could see that I had put up a wall to guard against anything having to do with the spiritual and alternative world.

Anyway, the fact that I was not really back on my feet after three months of intensive care with my beloved massage therapist's gentle hands, made me a bit scared. My companion, pain, hadn't really been willing to leave me quite as rapidly as I had hoped. Hanne suggested that I probably carried around more in my body than she could handle with her massage. So she offered to connect me with her mother.

Hanne's mother was no ordinary mum, she was a Rosen therapist, a therapy where the therapist's hands are guided to soothe the patient's inner wounds. This therapy opened up doors to my inner world in a way I had not experienced before, and I am forever grateful I found this gentle but strong method of understanding all the memories and scars left on my body throughout my life.

Another thing Rosen therapy opened up for me was the ability to speak in public about my inner feelings. I can't tell you how terrified I was the first time. I am sure I am not alone in this feeling. I've become aware of how keeping things inside — alone, deep and dark, so no one else can see — is literally killing people. At best, it is making people suffer through their life, feeling all sorts of guilt, shame, and horrific feelings, just because of who they are, or what they have experienced. It doesn't necessarily have to be their own fault that they ended up in the situation, but they still carry the shame and blame for it. And having overcome my fear, I feel passionate about helping others find their voice as well.

But there was more lurking in the still water around the treatment I got in my first Rosen therapy course. I met the most beautiful artist. She shared her personal story with me, and when I realized she had become a late bloomer professional artist, I felt a light was lit inside me. It made me remember how much I enjoyed drawing and painting when I was younger. She had a painting with her to light up the event, and I bought it. Along with the painting I received a mentor who helped me kick-start my own painting career.

A whole new life was opening up before my eyes, and I was amazed to find out that I could spend so much time in front of a canvas watching the colors blend without having to look after my long-time companion, pain. Painting was something new, something totally different. In the beginning I had a hard time defining what it really meant to me. Looking back, I see that art is a gift the universe has given to me. It had given me pain for so many years, and now it wanted to give me pain*ting* instead.

In a perfect world, one would hope that life became one happy journey after such an epiphany. But in a way, I'm actually happy to tell you it was not. I have had to go through a lot, even after what I've told you. There have been things that have almost killed me mentally, but I have managed to stand tall. Not because I am stronger, but because I am more vulnerable now, and I'm aware of it. I know where to go and who to turn to when I feel lost. I know I am provided for and I have faith in the fact that as long as I follow the path of flow I will find the right way out of each situation.

I've had times of insecurity. I've had the feeling of not being good enough, feeling I should have gone to an art school in order to proclaim myself an artist. I felt that I, with my background, didn't have the 'right' to say I am a painter. But what can I say except that I know exactly how the painting should look when I see it. And until I get to that phase, I follow my intuition and let myself be led by forces I do not master. I show up in front of the canvas, lift the pencils, and then wait for the universe to provide me with the X-factor. It works!

What I have managed to understand is that I have developed myself into an artist and people want to buy my paintings. I have held successful exhibitions and I am now welcoming clients to come paint with me. And this is not something my ego needs to brag about, it just is what it is, and I am happy to share it with other emerging artists.

Below are my top 11 tips to survive trauma that I really want to share with the world:

1. I am not a victim.(And neither are you!)
2. I can create the life I want by setting clear intentions.
3. I am the only person in the world that knows what is best for me, therefore, I need to take care of myself.
4. I need to put myself first, in order to be able to help others (Remember that metaphor from airplanes? You have to put on your own mask first!)
5. The only one I can change is myself.
6. Get rid of and set boundaries with people who are harmful to you. You can't allow people to intrude on your life, and you can't blame anyone else for not taking the actions you need to thrive.
7. You will become (or you already are) more or less like to 5-6 people you spend the most time with. So if you want to change, you may need to change your environment.
8. Stop comparing yourself with others, and stop dwelling on what others think or say about you. What they say about you

is only a reflection of themselves and their own thoughts, and has nothing to do with you.

9. Find the things in life that you love doing so much that you cannot NOT do them.
10. Regardless of what you do in life, remember to have fun and look for joy.
11. It surely helps to think positive… so be mindful about the words you use about life.

From being a climber, a fighter, a person that was so obsessed with showing people I could master any game, and win them all, I have turned into a person who wants to speak about love; to speak about trust. I want to lift people up, show them they have the answers within themselves.

The one thing to start believing in, in this world, is your own inner voice. If you have never listened to it before, it takes some effort to find it and start believing in the signals and the pushes your body is sending you. My body sent me pain, it has been a hard fight, and not something I really recommend. Looking back, I see that the pain pushed me towards finding a better life for myself. Pain helped me tap into my superpower, painting, and I have a feeling you can find yours as well. My hope is that once you find your way, you will unlock your superpower that no one can take away from you.

In my newly established painting courses I teach about finding your own superpower through your own painting style. When you've finished class you should feel that you have everything you need inside of you, and start believing that "I am perfect and lovable just as I am."

I so want people to see this for themselves and start spreading the love to the world.

About the Author

Stine Moe Engelsrud is spreading the word about what art can do for you in your recovery process; finding the way back to being the real and true you. Her vision for the future is to create a space where people can come and talk about life with real people about real problems and, at the same time, engage with art.

Stine's art is proudly featured on the back cover of this book.

You can connect with on social media:
facebook.com/ArtbySME
instagram.com/smengelsrud

None of Us Were Built to Be Robots

Taz Thornton

Trauma can be one of the most powerful transitionary phases of our lives. Finding the proverbial light at the end of that tunnel, moving through, and rebuilding — it can be utterly transformative. The original power-through-pain experience.

This isn't the space to go into great detail (I'd need an entire book for that!) but let me tell you that trauma and I are old friends. I've been through domestic abuse, deep grief, debt, depression, and suicidal desires that resulted in a wrecked car and a broken back. Suffice to say, I hit a wall — total breakdown.

I've had my heart, mind and soul shattered and rebuilding was one of the most healing experiences of my life. I still believe my breakDOWN was my breakTHROUGH.

For a while, I was terrified of going back there. I was so afraid of that black dog of depression sinking his teeth into me again that I suspect – on some level – I was unwittingly calling him. Though I can only really see this in retrospect, I think I spent some time trying to turn off my emotions – attempting to dull the pain in order to keep moving forward.

Today, as I have been able to turn things around and use my own experiences to coach, support and inspire others, I'm noticing some trends and beliefs that I'm finding a little bit worrying – and I think those of us who have come through tough times might be even more susceptible.

Let me explain…

I want to tell you something really important, something that might fly in the face of words from positivity coaches and happiness 'gurus' the world over.

What I want to share might just rock you to the core… or it might help you to feel freer than ever, as if some invisible weight has been lifted from your heart.

Are you ready? Brace yourself, here it comes…

Nobody is happy and joyful 24/7, and I don't believe we should ever aim to be.

We are not robots. We are human beings, and that makes us capable of experiencing all kinds of emotions: ups, downs and everything in between.

There's a worrying trend in today's personal development 'movement' – often made worse by the continual 'likes' on Facebook and Instagram. We are quick to consume all those positive quotes as well as those little videos with a core message of hope, but despite their so-called encouraging messages, we often find ourselves living a 'surface level life'. Sometimes, that can be the wisest move as a short-term coping mechanism, but it's not sustainable long-term.

What worries me is that we're forgetting it's okay, sometimes, to not be okay. If we've been through trauma in the past, this is particularly understandable, and that's why I was moved to write this.

We need to be able to hold onto the lessons from whatever challenges life delivered for us, without holding onto the pain. We also need to be able to trust that we have the ability, the support and the tools we need to move into the future without attempting to flick that switch and disconnect from our emotions.

I'm seeing society pulling further and further away from the of heart and processing everything with the brain.

Back in the world of social media, those 'uplifting' quotes on pretty backgrounds get scanned, sorted and stored somewhere in our heads, and we unwittingly start programming ourselves to hold onto optimism at all times. If we're not careful, we start to create heart/mind disconnect.

Don't get me wrong, positivity and optimism absolutely rock, but when we start to create a comfort zone where we believe we should always, always be smiling and sniffing gaily at the flowers of life, our own internal computer will do whatever it takes to action that command — even if that means turning off, or dulling, our emotions.

For me, this becomes even more important to understand and notice after trauma when, arguably, we'll be doing everything we can to avoid getting lost in that confused tangle of feelings again. It's my belief that we're at risk of treating our emotional bodies in the same way so many of us treat someone going through grief. I'm sure you will have witnessed this… maybe you've been an active participant.

Picture the scene: someone we love is grieving, for someone or something, and they're desperately upset. We hate seeing those we care about hurting, so we do everything we can to distract them, keep them busy, keep them away from that flood of tears we don't want to see, tears we don't want them to experience.

We *think* we're doing a good thing. We're doing everything in our power to keep them upbeat whilst we're with them but, in fact, all we're doing is delaying that grief and leaving them to go through it alone, long after we've closed the door and skipped away, happy in the knowledge that we've done our good deed for the day and kept that smile in place.

The important thing to remember is that our behaviour comes from a good place, so it's something for us to learn from, not something to beat ourselves up over.

Grief is a normal part of life. Held in balance, it's also a healthy part of life. It's part of the shedding of old to make way for new. We can't invite in those new, positive emotions and life experiences if our human body storage unit is still crammed full of grief.

We need to stop trying to distract people away from grief and, instead, help them to hold that space in a clean, balanced way; we need to support them through the tears and, when the time's right, support them in rediscovering, and inviting in their happiness too.

That makes sense, right? Good.

Now try applying that rule to yourself. Instead of trying to force yourself into a permanent state of bliss, learn to honour and respect the undulating nature of emotions.

Holding onto a positive attitude isn't so much to do with always being happy, but in having the tools, outlook and objectivity to not stay in that space of depression for longer than we 'need' to. It's not about never having a down day; it's about choosing not to set up home in that space.

My journey back to wholeness included deep soul searching, spiritual exploration and 'mind-glue', including meditation, energy medicine, neuro linguistic programming and, most power-full (hyphen deliberate) of all, work with shamans and medicine people. Sure, I took the anti-depressants too, but it was the non-tangible medicine that saved my life, restored my soul and convinced me to say 'yes' to life and really LIVE.

A very human reaction to going through anything traumatic can be to do everything in our power to avoid that scenario in future. I know this first hand, and it's one of the reasons our society's tango with head-heart disconnect worries me.

These days, I use many of my own experiences to support and inspire others, which is how I'm able to recognise these patterns and write about them here, in this book. Through my work, I hear so many people using phrases such as "I just keep myself busy so I don't go there," or "I lose myself in Facebook for a while," or "I keep remembering this positive quote and reminding myself that life could be so much worse, and I feel really guilty if I feel sad now."

Beautiful people (and yes, that IS you — every one of us is beautiful), we should never feel guilty, or shameful, about feeling sad. I understand; I truly, deeply do, but we cannot avoid ever feeling upset.

Remember the grief scenario? Can you see how we're in danger of creating that same situation in our own lives? If we don't allow those less than joyful emotions breathing room, when will they come out? How will they come out?

If we don't handle things safely and sanely, holding the energy and remembering the beauty and perfection of who we are, trapped emotions have the power to distort in order to force their way out.

It's too easy to look at others – particularly in the social media world – fall into the comparison trap and assume it's all okay for them. Since I've stepped further into the public eye, people have frequently leapt to all kinds of conclusions about me: I live in a mansion, I drive a Ferrari, I'm constantly happy, have lots of money and possess THE perfect life.

Here's the truth: I live in a three-bed semi, I drive a Citroen, I'm happy much of the time, have more money than I had this time last year (which was more than the same time the year before) but I still don't have a massive savings pot and still worry when an unexpected bill hits. I have the perfect life for me RIGHT NOW, but that's a long way away from society's idea of 'perfect'.

As I write this, from my heart, I'm just coming out of a two-day downer. I've felt spiky, angry, depressed... and more than a little fearful because part of me recognised this state felt far too much like home.

Know what tripped me? My wife and I have just returned from a fabulous few days in a castle, supporting some dear friends who were getting married. It was a glorious, amazing adventure. Between times, I was able to do some wonderful spirit and energy work in the castle, soak up amazing gardens and connect with some stunning trees and wildlife. In many ways, our trip was idyllic.

Ready for the rub? We also got to spend time with another dear friend who, through the circumstances of her life, has ended up with a potentially life-changing sum of money. I am genuinely happy for her; it's been a rocky road and she utterly deserves this. But... by the time I was on my way home, those old gremlins were biting and I'd fallen into a pattern of comparison and inadequacy, wondering if I really was 'good enough' to make it and panicking about running out of years and not being able to create a stable enough environment for my family.

This is an old, outdated thought cycle for me – it taps into those times of trauma, during which I leapt from a high-powered, top-level corporate career in order to save my life and rebuild. My wife has always been wonderfully supportive, so this thought pattern is absolutely all my own and speaks to 'throwing away' a lucrative career in favour of 'naval gazing'. It's all total tosh but, years back, when we were going through far tougher times, this was the stick I used to beat myself with frequently.

When we actually got home, we realised we had no hot water. Our boiler was flashing with a fault light (quite frankly, it's probably nearing the end of its life). A new boiler to replace ours won't be cheap and it's not a cost we've accounted for. Of course, this all added to the garbage being spouted by the 'money monkey' in my head.

Add this to being tired after a very long journey, a little hormonal and a bit under the weather, as well as being worried about my mom's health at the moment, and I was heading downwards on the emotional helter-skelter and not enjoying the ride at all.

I tried everything in my kit bag to shift my mood. I sang. I exercised. I dug out my ukulele and tried to learn some new songs. I meditated. I journeyed. Nothing seemed to work. And then I couldn't sleep which, of course, made things worse.

Now, as I move away from that dip and notice my mood starting to climb, I can look back at the past few days and realise that, actually, EVERYTHING worked!

The singing helped to shift any blocks from my communication chakra, which stopped me closing down and being unable to express what was happening for me.

The exercise got my endorphins moving and stopped me plummeting into an even darker place with no ladder.

The ukulele practice tapped into part of my brain I probably hadn't been using properly for a while, so it gave me something else to concentrate on, whilst not tipping into total avoidance. Plus, I was creating music (arguably), so making something positive and upbeat.

The meditation helped me to find a little piece of inner calm in the midst of all that chaos and, of course, helped me to zone out and away from 'Miserable Money Mind Monkey'.

The journey helped me to take note of old patterns, brought me support and healing from my guides *and* provided me with a little insight into ancestral patterns I need to work on.

If I hadn't been able to use all those tools, who knows where I'd be right now.

Now, as my mood rises, I'm gaining a sense of perspective and I'm feeling so, so grateful for everything I have.

I'm reminded that last time we had an issue with our plumbing system, I had to go cap in hand to an uncle and take a loan to replace our burst water tank, and then go through all the needless emotions of shame and dismay when he chased for repayment faster than I'd been able to make up the cash. This time, I won't have to do that. I'll have to juggle some and manifest more income quickly to make up the shortfall, but I know I can do that. Last time, it was winter and bitter cold. This time, we have no hot water in summertime, so the urgency isn't so great. I'm thankful for that.

The other huge piece of perspective I'm taking from this – and I really hope you will be able to take this on board as well – is that my downer didn't last long. I was in a slump for a couple of days, and I was actively building a ladder throughout that time.

I didn't try to avoid feeling 'down', attempt to switch my feelings off or ignore them. Instead, I set out to change them – to flip my negatives into something more positive.

With this many years' post-trauma perspective, I can look back and see why I hit that brick wall. I can see why I wanted – and tried – so desperately to die, why I used to pray for an illness to take me away from this planet, why I ended up so broken.

Remember what I said earlier about trapped emotions distorting to find a way out? That's precisely what happened. I didn't know how to convey what I was going through. I didn't want to appear vulnerable. I didn't want to admit how unhappy I was, how trapped I felt. So, I chose to say nothing.

NO-thing distorted into SOME-thing. And that 'something' distorted into a life with walls that felt to be closing in and a misguided belief that everyone in my world would be far better off without me in it.

How wrong could I have been? If I'd been successful in any of my bids to check out of life back then, think how much I would have missed, how many people I would have never have been able to help, how many lives I could never have been able to save simply by sharing my own story.

If you've been through trauma, if that's why you're reading this book, please, please understand that no matter what you've been through, disconnecting from your emotions won't be a great coping mechanism long-term. Be mindful when you're browsing social media and soaking up all those quotes and all that chatter. How are you feeling? How is it affecting you? Is it really useful? Would it benefit you to get outdoors and away from the screen for a while? And yes, it really is okay to not be smiling all the time… not even sleeping with a coat hanger in your mouth would achieve that state properly.

Please don't busy away your life in a bid to avoid thinking about what happened for fear of being bitten by the black dog again. Find someone to help, support and guide you if you need to, but remember that it does get better, the down times get shorter and every one of your emotions is there for a reason – even the sadness; just don't invite it to fill your heart 24/7.

One more thing... one of the greatest ways to flip those negatives and move beyond trauma is to use your own experiences to help, inspire and inform others. It's become almost the default setting for me now: 'Ooh – that was challenging. How can I use what I learned to help someone else?'. You might say that's precisely what I've been doing with this chapter.

Until next time,

#UnleashYourAwesome,

Taz

x

About the Author

Taz Thornton is a motivational speaker who trained with the same team as Tony Robbins - so don't be surprised if she gets you fire walking! Her unique blend of 'tribal' communication tools learned from shamanic cultures, NLP skills and years in top-line management means she can get right to the issues holding you back.

A TEDx speaker, best-selling author, visibility specialist and award-winning empowerment coach, Taz gets people speaking honestly like you've never known.

Connect with me! I'm on most of the popular social platforms. #UnleashYourAwesome

www.TazThornton.com
Email: Taz@TazThornton.com

How Depression Changed My Life

Stephan Conradi

Hello, my name is Stephan Conradi and I would like to tell you an intimate story about my life.

In 2005 I graduated from the Sport University Cologne in Germany. My dream was always to live a free and independent life so I left Germany for 7 months to learn Spanish in Guatemala. After coming back and working in Germany for a little while I realized that Germany would definitely not be my future home. So in 2008 I went to the Spanish island of Mallorca with my girlfriend Caroline and established an outdoor sport activity business. We did some country hopping for several years to survive financially, spending the summers in Spain and winters in Germany.

After some time it started to be very stressful for me and I began to have trouble sleeping. I ignored the symptoms for a while until it was unbearable. Due to the fact that my health insurance was in Spain it was tricky to consult a German doctor. The waiting list was 3 months or longer, so I ended up looking for someone in Spain. Finding a trustworthy doctor can be difficult, so I "tested" various doctors, but had little success.

Nobody close to me would believe that I was suffering with depression, because my life looked just to sunny and "perfect" in the eyes of the outside world. It was in 2014 when my stress was so overwhelming that it seemed as if my emotions disappeared completely. Some people call it a disconnection from your heart. My body's ability to create normal feelings had ceased to function. I fell into a deep resting mode and I was incredibly fearful. Fear was the only thing I felt. That was the first time that doctors confirmed a depression diagnosis. This created an even bigger discomfort in me because I did not know if the depression would ever end.

Now looking back, I would describe this situation like being in a big tank of mud. I imagined myself sinking down low, my mouth and nose covered to the point of not breathing. Luckily I started to float, so that it was just possible to inhale through my nostrils. Looking up, I saw that the tank was a couple of metres high. How could I get out of here?

It took about 6 months in the summer of 2014 to get out of that dark and muddy tank of depression and I used a lot of different techniques and methods to do so. All the doctors I contacted to help me during that dark time ended up giving me medication and some superficial conversations. It made life a little bit better for me, but the drugs made me numb and I felt continuously unsatisfied, because I knew that this was not a sustainable solution. I missed the feeling of a true curative process and I was not happy with having to always suppress my symptoms. There was no progress in the therapy that I had been offered. I could not feel myself getting better, which I missed a lot. But I realized very well what the medication did for me, it was OK, but not enough.

I had a long and deep conversation with Caroline one night while the kids slept. The next day I knew that I had to change something. I stopped taking the medication although this was highly NOT recommended. Neither my doctor nor my closest family knew about it, but I felt that this was the only way out. More and more, I realized that I had to take responsibility for my situation so I put my best effort into finding methods that would get me out of this gloomy mood. I realized that I needed to help myself. I am self-taught and always loved to learn when I found things interesting or helpful. So I consumed a variety of resources, including Mindfulness Based Stress Release, meditation, yoga, several books, breathing meditation, podcasts, music and videos.

I spent time analyzing which moments were the best for me and which times in my life I appreciated the most. Spending time in or close to water, like the sea, always gives me a relaxed and safe feeling. Therefore I used the water in combination with breathing meditation as a relaxation tool, which still is one of the best ways for me to calm my mind and body.

I also connected with people in my social networks with similar health issues and was surprised how many others of similar age were suffering with depression. It was a relief to know that others are on a similar path and I was always very curious to hear how they got out of their situation.

I found mindfulness very helpful for me, though focusing on only one action at a time, to keep the focus on one single thought is still challenging for me. I do have a sort of "monkey mind" with plenty of things popping up in my head which need to be controlled first, otherwise my physical actions would be also out of control. So I followed a mindfulness course over a couple of weeks during a winter on Mallorca, which was very helpful. Unfortunately, when the course ended, I did not continue practising it.

During the weeks after my first depressive period I kind of felt a resilience growing within me that made me feel unstoppable and resistant from any other depressions. I felt very confident and thought that nobody nor anything else could ever hurt me again. When I had my medical treatment in 2014, the doctor told me that 50 percent of people who suffer with depression will go through another depression in life again. At that time, just recovering from my first depression, I thought: This will DEFINITELY not happen to me! But I learned another lesson a few months later in spring 2017. A couple of stressful events happened at the same time and I lost control over my life again.

When it hit me the second time, I had the same feeling as the first episode. External situations seemed to create a lot of stress within me, kind of dragged me down and gave me the feeling of losing control. So I fell into the mud bucket again, but this time a little bit differently. It was not as deep this time. I was covered in mud only up to my chin. So breathing was possible through my mouth and nostrils, and I knew that I could get out of this situation. So I used my methods and techniques more intensively and also had a lot of personal support from family and my staff. A few months later, I started feeling better.

I now follow a strict, daily routine which helps me to maintain some regularity and balance. I start most of the days with my favourite music, breathing meditation and some yoga poses. Being physically close to water or floating at the water's surface is the "whipped cream" of my mental health. Water always gives me a comfortable feeling.

Gaining New Insights

At one point I asked myself, 'What is the story behind depression for me? Why did I go through this again and what do the two calls mean to tell me?' The two depression periods meant to me that I was simply not doing the right things *for me*. Although I created the business myself I kind of grew out of it. After a couple of years running the business I noticed that we did well, but that I became more and more unhappy with what I did every day. I felt a potential in me, that I could not properly live while running the business as an owner and CEO.

The winter of 2017/18 was very strange in terms of my physical health. It started with an ordinary cold in December 2017 which landed me in the hospital with a lung infection. Then an ear infection and a painful ruptured eardrum followed in the spring. I had all of this happen while lying in bed. It felt if someone had pierced my eardrum with a needle and I ended up crawling on the floor because the pain was so overwhelming. I lost my hearing almost completely on the injured ear and I had the typical symptoms of a traumatised eardrum including vertigo and blood running out of my ear.

Just a few weeks later, while having a Sunday morning discussion with my 3 year old, she put her index finger into my right eye. She was cosy in bed with her mom and there was no arguing or verbal fight. Looking back I have the feeling that I was just physically too close to her. It was a pretty intense pain and I immediately fell to my knees and covered my eye. A few moments later I went to the bathroom to soothe the eye with cold water. Over the day it did not get better, it teared a lot and I couldn't see properly. About 24 hours later I went to see a doctor. He was pretty upset with me for waiting so long. He diagnosed a corneal injury.

A couple of weeks later I started to have symptoms of neurodermitis, an itchy skin condition, and I thought, 'what is this all about?' There were so many physical signals, which I obviously did not interpret well. But what I noticed very well was that during the time of having all these physical issues my senses changed. I now hear, taste and perceive things differently. But only if I am in a kind of "perceiving mode." On the other hand I can ignore things quite well, if I am busy with my thoughts for example.

One morning in June 2018 we traveled to a family birthday. I noticed the birds singing in the morning and I was very surprised that they never stopped during the day. At home in Spain the birds start singing at around 5:30 am in summer and the singing normally ends about an hour later. In earlier days I would have never paid attention to this.

My sense of taste also changed a lot. I do not like ordinary food from the typical mass supermarkets any more. I prefer not to eat vegetables or any other groceries, until they have the 'right' taste for me. I do enjoy the fruits and veggies from the local farmers on the island a lot. Furthermore, I almost lost my appetite for meat and alcohol and I appreciate eating vegetarian way more than before the illness. Even Nutella does not mean much anymore, which is a BIG thing for me.

Probably the weirdest change I've noticed is my brain activity. I have the impression that I think faster since the depressive periods. Switching between my 3 languages daily is quicker. And my physical activities seem to be faster and more effective. If you would ask my partner Caroline, she might say that I changed to a completely different person.

An Invitation

During the spring of 2018, I received an interesting invitation via a newsletter by Stig Severinsen. Stig holds a couple of world records in freediving and created "Breatheology," a movement that teaches people to breathe better and live a healthier life. This newsletter was an invitation to the European Transformational Teachers Gathering in Alicante, Spain.

This was my road back, the road back to me and the values that had been covered and not been lived for quite some time. To go to this wonderful seminar was like a reward for me. Steinar

Ditlefsen, the founder, promoted the seminar with a strong claim: "This seminar is made for creating deep connections between people. An event to create long term relationships between the audience."

At the time I did not believe Steinar because this sounded kind of impossible to me. That is, until I went to Alicante and felt what was going on there. Around 100 seminar participants joined the event and I took a chance to talk to approximately 15 people. I had wonderful encounters with all of them. It seemed as if we were all speaking the same language. I realized that we had very similar reasons for coming to this heart driven seminar. It was very surprising to me that I connected so easily with everyone I talked to.

While at the seminar, I met one woman, to whom I connected a little bit differently. She was from Norway and other seminar participants told me that she could heal through her eyes. *Really?* I found this to be insane and a bit spooky at the same time. I met her one evening and she told me the first evening that she did not really understand the purpose of coming to this event. She had been invited by a friend and wanted to deny the invitation but someone at work convinced her to come. During our conversations, for just a couple of minutes, we finally figured out the reason. I had the strong feeling to meet her again the next day.

The second evening, we ended up talking with the most beautiful farewell words that I heard so far. I said: "Thank you very much for coming," because I knew that at least one of her reasons for coming to this event was me. She had looked into my eyes and I could feel that she changed something within me. She opened my eyes so I could see myself better. And this was basically the confirmation to follow my heart and just be myself.

She replied to my farewell words: "Thank you very much for bringing me here." This is something I will never forget and since then I am deeply connected not only to her, but also to the movement of these people who all came to Alicante and are all on a very similar mission.

I am happy to report that I am back on track. I am creating my new path since that event in spring 2018. At this point I would like to offer big thanks to Stig Severinsen, Steinar Ditlefsen, Paul Luftenegger, Dr. Andrea Pennington and my Norwegian "eye healer." All have a great way of seeing life and the world and they follow incredible visions. I already learned so much from them and feel super grateful.

My Vision for the Future

Now I can see my two deep periods of 'sinking' as a blessing because I understand how to interpret them. I've come to realise that the deeper you are, the higher everything is around you. There is no high without a low, and I do believe that there are so-lutions for any kind of problem. Accepting the current situation and believing in yourself and a positive change might be the first steps to get out of the gloomy mood.

Now, with this big treasure in my hands, I am going to create something be-a-U-ti-ful. I want to be on stage to share my experi-ences to reach as many people as possible. Currently I am also creating an online course to support others in changing their mindset and paradigms for more relaxed living. I am also very passionate about learning. That's why I am going to host and or-ganize events on Mallorca with partners. I would like to become an eye opener to many people.

We all have our problems, history and background. But no matter what has happened, I do believe that we can change our lives for the better. I also believe that we should take responsibility for ourselves. It's everybody's duty to be happy. Focus on yourself first and then share your bliss, gratefulness, love and whatever makes you and other people happy.

Through my experience with illness, I developed an understanding and appreciation for the beauty of life. All one needs is to listen and see it. A lot of people these days are too influenced by too much information. We have too many things and information coming towards us.

The solution and answer to our questions lie within us, we just need to listen. I know it needs some practise and some time to implement into your life. But it's worth it, because you will end up living more relaxed, happy and less fearful. The first step is to create an awareness. Now that I turn on the flight mode of my phone several times a day, I live much more relaxed. It can be that simple.

If you want to join my mission to change people's minds and paradigms to live an easier and more relaxed life, please follow me:

www.stephanconradi.com
www.facebook.com/pleaseshine
www.instagram.com/stephanconradi

Recovering from Caregiver Burnout

Andrea Pennington, MD, C.Ac.

I previously shared part of the story I'm about to tell you in a book called Resilience Through Yoga and Meditation. My chapter explored how compassion and meditation helped me recover from a draining few months as a full time caregiver to my elderly mother. Now, three years later I have new insights on how illness can set us on a path to new life. I am more convinced than ever that the practice of self-compassion and meditation can help us develop resilience and provide relief for a whole host of other big and small crises.

The Calm Before the Storm

I had the pleasure and luxury of creating a deep meditation practice for several years in response to following my heart and moving to France in 2010. (As I explained in Part 1 of this book, Surviving Suicide). Sitting on the beach, meditating in the countryside and becoming grateful for life's beauty became my soul nurturing rituals long before I really needed them. Becoming more mindful and compassionate helped me deal with frequent minor life frustrations — such as dealing with the French administration, traveling to multiple countries with a small child and running a global media company from Europe.

Meditation, QiGong, aerobic exercise and being in nature with lots of sea and sun have helped me stay upbeat and optimistic. I believe they keep the ugly monster of depression at bay, something I experienced for most of my life.

I'll offer my advice to you right up front here — rather than waiting until your life is falling apart, your mental outlook is down the drain or you lose a loved one, I suggest you make meditation a regular part of your healthy lifestyle, so that over time you build up resources to cope with life's many challenges and if you're in need of an emergency rescue, meditation may be just what the doctor ordered.

Mom's Diagnosis: Alzheimer's Dementia

About seven years ago my siblings and I all expressed how obvious it was that Mom was becoming more forgetful and easily confused. Over the last few years each of us saw a dramatic and rapid decline in both her short term memory and daily functioning. It was tough for us to come to terms with the fact that our mother, who had been a sought-after, brilliant physician, was now at the age of 83, asking us the same basic questions every five minutes. To make matters more challenging, Mom is also nearly blind now due to a long history of glaucoma and she is often in physical pain due to arthritis.

In the early stages of her dementia she experienced frequent mood swings. Mom has always been feisty, but soon we watched her go from snappy and irritable to weepy and blue in a matter of minutes. Needless to say, this became quite a challenge for my sister and brother who were Mom's primary caretakers.

A visit to the Cleveland Clinic Center for the Brain led to the inevitable diagnosis of dementia, most likely the Alzheimer's type[2]. Like so many people with a family member diagnosed with

---

[2] I say most likely because you cannot officially diagnose Alzheimer's disease without looking at brain tissue under the microscope. Short of a brain biopsy, which nobody living wants to do, the only way to know for sure requires a brain analysis after death.

dementia, my initial reaction was to jump into rescue mode. As a physician who specialized in longevity medicine, I suggested we bring an arsenal of 'smart drugs' into play. These are the nootropics today's savvy bio hackers take starting in their 20s, whereas my wealthy executive clients began taking in their 40s to maintain sharp focus and to enhance brain function.

We tried a few of the medications approved for dementia which, unfortunately, had a host of side effects that were just unbearable for Mom. One pill got her too amped up. She would stay up all night long talking, and sometimes dancing! Another medication sharpened her thinking but sent her back in time to a period in her life where she owned a medical clinic. She would angrily yell that she was being mistreated and prevented from getting to work where she insisted that patients were waiting to see her. If she was particularly wound up, she could be heard talking to herself, counseling the imaginary patients who she 'saw' in front of her.

My sister and brother had alternated caring for Mom for a few years before their own signs of stress and overwhelm became so obvious that I was compelled to step in. It wasn't easy though. Over time my sister had become fiercely protective of Mom and often interpreted any help from me as a sign that she wasn't being trusted to care for her properly. For example, when I offered to fly from my home in the South of France to help them move into a new house, or to take mom on holiday for a few weeks, my sister defiantly said, 'No!' However, things became even stickier when I visited during the Summer of 2015 as it was clear that both my sister and my mother needed a break.

The Rescue

I've connected with other caregivers of aging family or spouses and I now have a greater understanding of how easily our lifestyle and household can crumble around us. Simple things that could easily be fixed are neglected while we care for someone who needs near constant attention. So many of us caregivers put our own needs last on the list — if they get on the list at all!

Though my sister rejected any physical help from me over the last two years I began to doubt my decision to stay away. When I arrived to visit I was beside myself. "I should have insisted," I agonized. I saw the full impact that assuming full responsibility for everything had on my sister. As a single working woman with no husband or other relatives nearby, the care taking role had become too much for my sister. And she rejected the idea of hiring an assistant to help out fearing that they might abuse Mom while my sister was at work. So Mom, who had always been so proud of her beautiful home, was now literally blind to the shabby conditions she lived in. This is when my guilt set in.

My mother was so happy to hug me and her granddaughter when we arrived and she pleaded for us to take her away. I felt so ashamed for not insisting on a visit sooner to unburden my sister from the full-time care taking responsibilities and I couldn't bear to see my mother so confined. So my daughter and I swooped in and agreed to take Mom on a jaunt half way across the map to my home on the French Riviera.

While waiting for Mom's passport to be renewed we spent a month together in the US and treated Mom to several outings and fun excursions. During that month I saw firsthand how fast Mom's memory and physical capacity was deteriorating. She was blind, immobile, confused. I felt sorry for her being now wheelchair-bound due to achy, stiff joints. In my mind it seemed like such a terrible state to be in. I was filled with compassion and felt compelled to do all that I could to both alleviate her suffering as well as provide as many enjoyable, love-filled moments as possible. Plus I wanted my daughter to have positive memories and happy moments with her grandma. So I went into overdrive — dinners, movies, miniature golf and ice cream.

Mom always loved Baskin & Robbins ice cream, in particular the flavor 'Pralines and Cream.' Having left the US eight years ago my daughter had never been to B&R, so while in Los Angeles I decided we'd have a Pennington girls bonding experience. After going through the drama of dressing Mom and putting on her wig and makeup (she was always a proud lady wanting to be seen looking good!) we descended the long flight of stairs to reach the car. I drove with such joy and anticipation as the sun was shining down on Mom's face in the passenger seat.

At the ice cream shop my daughter was filled with wonder at the vast numbers of ice cream flavors — 31 to be exact. As we sat down to enjoy our tasty treats Mom was in Heaven! I felt so pleased with myself. It felt like a positive accomplishment.

After gobbling down the delicious treats, we piled back into the car to head home, which was only about a 15 minute car ride. I pulled up, parked the car and just as Mom opened the door she says, "You know, I'd really love to have some ice cream."

She had completely forgotten the dreamy, ice-creamy bonding experience we just shared!

Undaunted, I comforted myself and reminded my daughter that even if her mind didn't store the memory at least her soul could recognize the effort that her daughter and granddaughter made to be fully present and loving.

The Descent

Mom was so delighted that she was going to be visiting France again, a country she loved and hadn't seen in over 25 years. Optimistic that the trip to Europe would bring Mom's spirits high, we packed up the wheelchair, her walking stick, medications and boarded our flight. If you think traveling with a small child is difficult, let me tell you, flying with someone who is confused, blind and forgetful is much harder! Needless to say, the plane ride was a horrendous nightmare and only a precursor of things to come. Mom did not believe that she was on an airplane. She insisted that she was in her home as she called out to everyone who passed by her seat. Suspicious that the passengers might be thieves, she tried to climb out of her seat and would reach across the aisle to touch the person sitting there to see who they were.

When we landed in France Mom was so disoriented she refused to leave the plane so the attendants had to carry her off as she resisted and yelled at them. The taxi ride home from the airport was equally embarrassing. She tried to climb into the front seat and begged the driver to let her out. She banged on the windows and called for the police to help her. Little did I know that my attempt to bring her joy and relief was only going to bring her — and me — sadness and misery.

With the time zone difference and Mom being totally disoriented, we stepped into a period of catering to her every need 24/7. Mom's anger and frustration for being out of her comfort zone led her to descend into a child-like tantrum on a daily basis. It's not hard to imagine the consequences: sleep deprivation, physical and emotional exhaustion, depression and yes, resentment.

Drawing on compassion and tolerance, my daughter and I persevered to keep Mom comfortable and entertained. But to no avail. I was worn down by her angry outbursts and nightly conversations with medical patients who didn't exist. Ultimately the fatigue and jabs at my wellbeing were too great. In my mind, I had given everything. My time, home, sleep, money, attention and care had been used and abused, not appreciated nor cherished, by the woman who gave me life. I was hurt by her lack of appreciation for what we sacrificed in having her in our home. Which made me feel ashamed for being so selfish! I was deflated and dejected.

Yet, what did I expect? Wasn't I the one who stepped in, posing as the heroic (codependent) savior, sacrificing everything for her? Was it realistic to think all would be rosy and well? After all, she is the one with a brain that is seemingly disintegrating before our very eyes. She is the one facing the last years of her life totally dependent on others, in pain and confused. Where did the unrealistic expectation that she would or could recognize how much we cared come from? And how could I be so damned selfish?

My Refuge — Meditating on Compassion

Realizing how bratty my internal dialogue had become, while hiding in the bathroom in shame and guilt, I broke down crying. My refuge and return to sanity came through my practice of meditation, specifically the Mettā, or loving-kindness meditation.

Mettā is a Pāli word that involves the desire that all living beings be well. It is more than just a feeling, it is an attitude of friendliness. From a Buddhist psychology perspective, if loving-kindness is directed towards our own suffering then self-compassion can arise, while if it is directed towards the suffering of others then compassion for them can develop.

To practice this meditation we begin by taking a few deep breaths to get centered and quiet. Then we begin with directing loving kindness toward ourselves. Sitting quietly, we mentally repeat, slowly and steadily, the following or similar phrases:

"May I be happy.

May I be well.

May I be safe.

May I be peaceful and at ease."

After directing loving-kindness toward ourselves, the practice involves holding the same kind intention toward people close to us, our loved ones and family. Next we extend the circle of compassionate wishes to people who are neutral, such as the grocery clerk, delivery guy or a random person we stand next to at the post office. Finally, we sit and direct compassion and the wish to ease suffering to difficult people, the ones in our life or in the world who seem particularly difficult to love.

I can tell you from personal experience this practice is profound. Beside the inner transformation that comes from finally being kind toward myself, I have recognized a clear shift in all of the relationships in my life. The loving-kindness meditation has grown in popularity among psychologists and therapists. Clinical research is finding the same results in a variety of different settings[3]. In clinical studies this meditation practice leads to an increase in positive emotions over time, which leads to an increase

---

[3] The benefits of reciting or thinking the simple phrases of the loving-kindness meditation improve love and social connections, too. A study in 2010 showed that participating in a 7-week loving-kindness meditation course helped to expand love and improved health on a personal level for participants.

in resilience resources, including mindfulness, self-acceptance, received social support, and positive relations with others.

Becoming more tolerant and compassionate to myself, allowed my heart and mind to reopen to offering true compassionate care to my mother. Through meditation we remember simple advice: just be present; that's the gift. As I eased my grip on internal expectations and released the tension of resisting what was happening, I found greater peace, and so did Mom. Her mood lightened significantly. I stopped telling her that her imaginary patients weren't there. I allowed her to enjoy the idea of being a helpful, caring physician, a role that had given her life tremendous significance. And the tension in the household was magically lifted.

As I relaxed into a solemn acceptance of Mom's condition, I could watch with wonder how she selectively relived certain memories from her early adult life in England. She recounted stories of her time in nursing school in London, the countries she visited, the men she dated (despite her family's disapproval), and the adventure she embarked on with her immigration to the United States. She expressed great pride and satisfaction while recounting stories of her time at medical school when I was just a baby. She beamed with joy and satisfaction at a life lived with no regrets.

Mom often told me how happy she was with her life. Yes, she said she wished there was a man to romance her — even at age 83! And yes, she wished she had more to give to her children and granddaughter as an inheritance. But she told us, on more than one occasion, that she felt a deep sense of satisfaction and pride

Cohn, Michael A., and Barbara L. Fredrickson. "In Search of Durable Positive Psychology Interventions: Predictors and Consequences of Long-Term Positive Behavior Change." The journal of positive psychology 5.5 (2010): 355–366 that during her illustrious lifetime, she had done "her Master's work" to the best of her ability. She often said, "when I cock up my toes and go to the great Beyond, I shall hear 'Job well done!' And that's all that matters to me now."

The Resilient Rebound

Through meditation and becoming fully present and accepting of the current circumstances, I came to terms with my own attachment to a desire for her to be 'well' again. I had to let go of my clinging to the vision of the Mom I grew up with and looked up to. A newfound acceptance and appreciation of the frailty of life emerged.

I renewed my personal boundaries and recommitted myself to my own compassionate self-care routines including lots of meditation breaks, hot baths, movies on the couch with my daughter and long walks in nature. Rather than sleeping with one eye open and jumping up every time Mom started chatting, I decided to give in to peaceful sleep and allow her to talk to imaginary people through the night. Instead of rushing home to supervise her every meal and movement, I hired a caretaker to come in during the day so that I could continue my outdoor exercise routine.

Allowing myself time in nature to breathe and reconnect with Life, I slowly let go of the need to 'fix' Mom. And I allowed myself to become mindfully aware and grateful for life.

The Resolution

The resolution arrived only a few months later as I returned Mom to my sister's open arms back in America. I was relieved and sad at the same time. I feared that this might be the last time Mom recognized me. She seemed happy to be reunited with my sister, though she didn't realize that she hadn't been away from her for long.

On my last day I pulled out my laptop and we listened to my first TEDx presentation, the one I gave in Monaco about becoming who you really are. She listened with great attention and wonder. After hearing my 18-minute talk she told me that she could tell that I was 'doing my Master's work.' She expressed a sense of pride that was so gratifying to me, especially after so many years of yearning for acceptance and approval.

As I left for the airport the following day and hugged Mom and my sister goodbye I was at peace. I had fully accepted that I had done my best, in the eyes of myself and my soul, as well as in the eyes of Mom and my daughter.

I, of course, clearly saw the many errors of my ways. But I did not have any regrets. The choices I made felt right at the time. Given my own level of awareness and understanding I gave my all, with the best of intentions.

The experience allowed me to connect with my sister on a deeper level as well. And now she knows that she can call on me, even just to vent her feelings. And we both recognize the value in taking time for ourselves and how to laugh or shrug off the sometimes nutty things that happen with Mom. And we know that no matter what, we know that we can get through turbulent times and family crises with true grace and ease.

The Update

It has been 3 years since that tumultuous and traumatic summer. This year, when my daughter and I returned to visit my mother and sister we were fully equipped with compassion, patience and a willingness to be present with Mom as she is **now**.

Not carrying expectations or regrets allowed us to visit with her in a joyful and peaceful way.

Armed with lots of her favorite music we danced, we talked, introduced mom to vegan ice cream and we let her share what was on her mind. I was particularly struck by her new acceptance of her condition. She is in an advanced stage of dementia now and thankfully, she is more peaceful, grateful and focused on happy things. It was strange to see her turn down multiple offers to leave the house, have her pillow fluffed or her drinks re-heated. She told us that she was quite comfortable and so very appreciative of our presence.

I was deeply touched that after just a short while she pulled me close to say that she was doing so well that she wanted me to go. I was kind of shocked to hear her say, "You are young, you have your life to live now. You should be out there!" She gestured toward the door. She continued, "I'm doing well, I'm happy you came to visit, but I've lived my life, now it's time for you to go out and live yours."

I felt her giving me permission to live fully and continue my life in France and it brought tears to my eyes. By being present with her without expectation, she returned to the caring mother who wants the best for me.

Even in her fragile state my daughter and I received such precious love and attention, which is what we had intended to give to her. These are moments that have left such a strong impression on me.

The Lessons

To summarize but a few of the lessons the summer with Mom taught me.

- Life is precious. This human life is truly a gift to be cherished. We will be wise to live each day authentically, with purpose and always with the intention to give this life deep meaning.

- Life, as we know it, will end. So do not take youth for granted! Everything in this life is temporary and subject to change. We cannot escape pain, sickness, loss or death, so while you're here, nurture your body and brain. Enliven your heart and soul with adventure, love and fun. Savor the pleasurable experiences without clinging, knowing that all good things must come to an end. And resist the temptation to push away or fix every 'bad' thing. They, too, shall pass.

- Our behaviors determine the quality of our lives. The actions we take and choices we make are what bring forth the fruit of our lives, so be sure to generously choose love and compassion. Practice kindness and forgiveness to yourself as well as others. Cherish your ability to love freely, and often. Mom remembered her greatest loves, travels and triumphs — not the failures. She was able to say she lived with no regrets. Could you do the same?

- None of your possessions, jobs or accomplishments provide lasting comfort in themselves. And at the end of your life, none of them will go with you. So develop an open curious mind and heart while walking without attachment or resistance. Your determined focus on awakened living, serving others and evolving your mind and soul is paramount.

Andrea Pennington, MD, C.Ac
Cannes, France

You Are Not Alone

Jill Stocker, D.O.

Perhaps the four most powerful words anyone could ever hear are, "You are not alone."

We live in a society that is extremely "connected" technologically yet equally disconnected from one another. If you watch people walking on the street, no one is making eye contact, let alone even saying "Hello." If you watch people dining at restaurants, most are looking at their phone rather than their partner or family member. Everyone is gazing down at their phone, checking social media "connections" with people a world away, yet so very disconnected from not only themselves, but the person right in front of them. We're looking at how many "likes" we got for a post we delivered to the world, revealing the inner secrets of our minds and hearts; too afraid to communicate face to face, eye to eye about our feelings, our fears, our challenges.

In our hyper digitally connected world, we actually isolate ourselves and compartmentalize our thoughts, feelings, and emotions. Speaking up and out and connecting with another person takes away the power of those isolated, overwhelming thoughts. The act of simply saying to someone in their moment of need, crisis, angst, fear, anger, or overwhelm "You are not alone" robs those thoughts of their gripping negative energy.

In the words of the great Martin Luther King, Jr. "Our lives begin to end the day we become silent about things that matter."

The title of this book "Life After Trauma" can be a bit deceiving to some because sometimes it is the very trauma *of life* —

everyday life — things mounting and persisting and gaining momentum. It's not necessarily the typical "trauma" people think of, like a car accident or rape, that so strongly affects us.

It's the insidious nature of the disease of depression that so many, including myself, brush aside as "not that bad." Or we say "what do I really have to say and who really wants to hear about my not-that-important experience?"

Can you already feel how small someone can begin to feel because of all that negative self-talk? What's worse is all the negative talk from a spouse, friend or family member when you share something you're already sensitive and ashamed about. It can cause us to retreat to a nice safe hiding place called silence and isolation.

This was my world, until a few years ago, when I saw and heard a woman, physician, and public figure - Dr. Andrea Pennington - who I respected and admired. She spoke openly about *her* struggles with depression. I was literally dumbfounded. I had always been so fearful of speaking openly about my depression because I thought I would be perceived of as weak, incompetent, and a "victim." But when I heard Andrea speak, I had none of these thoughts. In fact, the only words that came to mind were **strong** and **courageous**.

We are only as sick as our secrets, and it is truly because of that one woman sharing her secret that I finally didn't feel so alone, ashamed, and like I had to hide. Her sharing her story unlocked my own self-imposed prison of my mind. Now, I find myself sharing quite openly with people about my struggles with depression and postpartum depression because I realize how much it actually helps us both. I also remember the horrible feeling of being so terminally alone, and I don't want anyone else to experience that unnecessarily.

My journey with depression and hormone imbalance started when I was in medical school. I began experiencing extreme mood swings around the time of my period. It wasn't what I had always thought of as "typical" depression; the picture I had painted of someone crying. I felt angry inside, and to avoid saying anything mean, I would just isolate myself. I had never heard anyone else share these types of feelings, so I kept them to myself, and was ashamed of them. It wasn't until a friend, who saw the isolation and a glimpse of the anger said, "You need to do something," that I sought help. I was actually mortified that she said this and shut down even more. I even started taking a "quick fix" pill to calm the crazy. It worked! Until it didn't.

I found myself having these feelings more often than just around my period, so I started taking medicine regularly — Prozac to be specific — to push down those feelings. I didn't even think to talk about it with someone. I didn't have time for that, I just needed to function!

I don't think feelings were ever a topic of conversation in my household. It was something that was handed down through the generations. My grandfather never even told by father he loved him until he was dying and in his 80s. This was the same man that, while I loved him dearly, gave me a swat instead of a hug when I was crying for a hug, homesick for my parents one summer, just a child. That's just the way things were…and is also how insidious "traumas of everyday life" gain momentum and urge us to continually seek cover.

So, I kept along this path of taking antidepressants, switching when they "stopped working" (meaning I either started having uncomfortable feelings or felt numb and dead inside). I remember one day vividly, returned home after a long day of seeing patients, I got down on the floor and literally laid there, just staring at the ceiling, while my kids played around me. This was not the kind of mother or person I wanted to be. This was not **living**!

With postpartum depression, it felt as if I were in a deep well that I was never going to get out of. I literally couldn't imagine being happy again. I felt so helpless and hopeless that I envisioned myself floating in my bathtub, dead, finally free of my agony. But I couldn't bear the thought of the pain that would cause my children. I was so horrified and ashamed that I had a suicidal thought – a fact I couldn't share until recently. I was in such a dark place that I even looked into electroconvulsive ("shock") therapy. I couldn't go on like that.

With the help of a few friends I finally opened up, only to discover they had similar feelings postpartum. I began seeing the light again. To know I wasn't terminally alone was such a relief, and I am thankful that they would reach out to me daily, to help pull me out of that well.

It wasn't until I began learning about my current specialty of hormonal optimization that I literally "woke up" to my life. I learned that many of my feelings were partially due to declining hormones, something I usually equated to hot flashes and night sweats. But then I remembered my mother going through her "change" and being suicidal, and that's when things really started shifting. Once I got my hormones optimized I began feeling "alive" again, with a newfound zest for life. I literally had lost the light behind my eyes, but still put the "I'm fine" mask on to present to the world. I realize now that I wasn't fooling anyone.

Then there was my first experience with meditation in a women's sharing circle. After a chanting meditation (which was a bit odd to me the first time) we went around the circle sharing what thoughts, feelings, and emotions had come up for each of us during the meditation. Again, I was dumbfounded, and shaking inside. I didn't think I was going to be able to speak. I had never heard anyone share the same fears, struggles, shame, sadness, and "not enoughness" as me so openly. I had felt terminally and uniquely alone in my struggles with depression, postpartum depression, divorce, verbal and emotional abuse, and extreme loneliness. And, right then, I finally didn't feel alone anymore.

It's been a long, arduous journey, and I'm still on it, uncovering old "traumas of everyday life." But with the help of others sharing their struggles, I have finally been able to acknowledge my own, heal them, and share them with others to continue this gift of connection, this gift of "You Are Not Alone." Even writing this right now I'm a little worried whether it's "Ok", or if it will make an impact at all. The reality is, it's *my* story and I can't fail at being "Me." The same goes for everyone else, including you.

What you have to say is important because it's *your* story, and you can't fail at being "You." It is when we are completely filleted, cut open and vulnerable that we are most authentically "us," which is what we truly should be with one another.

"There are, it may be, so many kinds of voices in the world, and none of them is without significance."

~ 1st Corinthians, 14th Chapter, verse 10.

I've learned, and am still learning, to express my feelings. But the interesting thing I've realized is that sometimes I don't even know what the feeling is I'm having because, for so long, I just shoved anything uncomfortable down, or was told I was "crazy" when I expressed myself, or it would come out as anger or rage. I have realized that the level of the anger I had was truly just the level of the pain and sadness I had covered for so long. Rather than FEELING it all those years - the pain and sadness, and understanding it - I FIXED it or hid it, until I couldn't anymore. I was so shut down because of the shame and fear of being "exposed" as an imposter, that I couldn't cry until nearly a year ago.

Now, when someone asks me how I'm doing, I no longer say "Fine," I say truthfully what I'm feeling because I have realized that in doing so, it not only helps me to be my authentic self, it also helps others be their's. I used to think as a doctor I had to have everything together and perfect…and that's just not so. So now, when I'm nervous about sharing in front of people, I don't get down on myself, I simply have compassion for that wounded inner child of mine and now allow others to see her.

If we would simply allow ourselves to communicate with the openness and innocence of a child, rather than the masks we feel we have to wear, there would be a lot less loneliness in this world.

I am not ashamed or embarrassed anymore because it's MY story, I own it, and I can't fail at being ME. I look at my everyday life traumas as gifts to clarity, authenticity, and connection that I can now share with others to empower them to be THEIR true selves.

I am happy to say my hormonal "awakening" has led to my spiritual awakening, and to my true, authentic Jill, unmedicated and with a full spectrum of emotions and feelings. No longer angry or dead inside. I am happier than I've ever been, and the light behind my eyes is at full force, helping to illuminate the road for others out of their darkness.

So whatever dark, painful, crazy feelings you may have bottled up inside, I want you to know: You Are Not Alone.

About the Author

Hi there! I'm Dr Jill. I'm not your traditional doctor. I specialize in Age Management Medicine and Hormonal Optimization. I've made it my life's work to help women (and men!) RECLAIM their sense of self, JUICINESS, EDGE, and VITALITY. As early as your late twenties, hormones that are VITAL to truly LIVING your life, start to decline and need to be corrected to get you back to the best YOU I know you can be. I'm here to help. My goal is to help you achieve the best version of yourself physically, mentally, emotionally, spiritually, and sexually!

I create a safe space to talk about things that are often deemed embarrassing or shameful, but are so crucial to our overall sense of self and being. I want to help you to truly take charge of your vitality and sexuality, to show you how to achieve the beautiful masterpiece of YOU!

Please find me here: *www.TheBodyWellUSA.com*

Conclusion

The stories in this book have probably opened your eyes to new possibilities. They certainly have done that for me. I hope that expanding your mind and exploring new ways to enhance your resilience will become a way of life for you now.

I sincerely wish you an inspired journey toward your beautiful life after trauma. If our paths should cross, I hope you will open up and share stories about your own experiences of resilience. Or perhaps you'll do so in one of my upcoming books or a live event?

Feel free to contact the brilliant, brave authors in this book. They are so heart-centered and precious, I know they will inspire you as they have me. Besides, being in the company of amazing people allows their special sauce to rub off on us, and if we let it, their magical qualities can also linger.

Here's to you,

Andrea and all of the authors of Life After Trauma

Please watch the #AskTheAuthor interview series by visiting www.MyLifeRewritten.com and sign up to receive special gifts from the authors.

About the Book's Creator

D r. Andrea Pennington is an integrative physician, acupuncturist, meditation teacher, and international speaker who is on a mission to raise the level of consciousness and love on our planet. As a personal brand architect, media producer, and communications specialist, she leverages her 20+ years of experience in broadcast and digital media to proudly help healers, Light workers and coaches to bring their brilliance to the world through publishing and media production with Make Your Mark Global Media.

Dr. Andrea is also a bestselling author, international TEDx speaker and documentary filmmaker. For nearly two decades, she has shared her empowering insights on vitality and resilience on the *Oprah Winfrey Show*, the *Dr. Oz Show*, iTV *This Morning*, CNN, the *Today Show*, LUXE-TV, Thrive Global and HuffingtonPost and as a news anchor for Discovery Health Channel. She also produced a four-part documentary series and DVD for Gaia entitled *Simple Steps to a Balanced Natural Pregnancy*.

Dr. Andrea has appeared in many print publications including *Essence, Ebony, Newsweek, The Sun, Red, Top Santé* and *Stylist*. She has also written or contributed to 10 books. As host of the talk show, *Liberate Your Authentic Self* and as founder of In8Vitality she blends her 'nerdy' mix of medical science, positive psychology, and mindfulness meditation to empower us all to show up authentically, love passionately, and live with vitality.

Visit Dr. Andrea online at:

AndreaPennington.com   RealSelf.Love

MakeYourMarkGlobal.com   In8Vitality.com

Get Social!

facebook.com/DrAndreaPennington

twitter.com/drandrea

linkedin.com/in/andreapennington

instagram.com/drandreapennington/

Other Books Published by Make Your Mark Global

Magic and Miracles: 21 Real Life Experiences from the Edges of Logic and Science Compiled by Andrea Pennington

The Magical Unfolding: 8 Magical Processes for Peace, Potential and Purpose by Helen Rebello

The Ultimate Self-help Book: How to Be Happy, Confident and Stress Free by Yvette Taylor

Finding Joy Beyond Childlessness by Lesley Pyne

I Love You, Me! My Journey to Overcoming Depression and Finding Real Self-Love Within by Andrea Pennington

The Orgasm Prescription for Women: 21 Days to Heightened Pleasure, Deeper Intimacy and Orgasmic Bliss by Andrea Pennington

The Book on Quantum Leaps for Leaders: The Practical Guide to Becoming a More Efficient and Effective Leader from the Inside Out by Bitta. R. Wiese

Turning Points: 11 Inspiring True Stories of Turning Life's Challenges into a Driving Force for Personal Transformation Compiled by Andrea Pennington

How to Liberate and Love Your Authentic Self by Andrea Pennington

The Top 10 Traits of Highly Resilient People by Andrea Pennington

Daily Compassion Meditation: 21 Guided Meditations, Quotes and Images to Inspire Love, Joy and Peace by Andrea Pennington

Eat to Live: Protect Your Body + Brain + Beauty with Food by Andrea Pennington

MAKE YOUR MARK GLOBAL

Get Published Share Your Message with the World

Make Your Mark Global is a branding, marketing and communications agency based in the USA and French Riviera. We offer publishing, content development, and promotional services to heart-based, soul-conscious authors who wish to have a lasting impact through the sharing and distribution of their transformative message. We can also help authors build a strong online media presence and platform for greater visibility.

If you'd like help writing, publishing, or promoting your book, or if you'd like to co-author a collaborative book, visit us online or call for a free consultation.

www.MakeYourMarkGlobal.com
+1(707)776-6310
andrea@MakeYourMarkGlobal.com

CPSIA information can be obtained
at www.ICGtesting.com
Printed in the USA
FSHW011415301218
54478FS